Story of the
Peace Garden State

by
Erling Nicolai Rolfsrud

Lantern Books
Route 1, Box 104
Farwell, Minnesota 56327
Phone 612-282-5876

Story of the Peace Garden State

Copyright, 1990
by
Erling Nicolai Rolfsrud

First printing, August, 1990

ISBN 0-914689-14-2

Printed in the United States of America
by
Echo Printing
Alexandria, Minnesota 56308

Dedicated
to those
with sodbuster spirit
past and present
and to the memory
of my immigrant homesteader parents
Nils and Rebecca Rolfsrud

CONTENTS

I—DAKOTA

1—The Land 1
2—The Prairie Primeval 2
3—Legend 3

II—THE FIRST PEOPLE

1—Indian Tribes in North Dakota 4
2—Uncle Buffalo 4
3—The Earthlodge Farmers 7
4—The Tepee Travelers 7
5—The Magic Wolf 9
6—The Birchbark Experts 9
7—The Clan 10
8—What the Indian Gave Us 12

III—THE FIRST WHITE MEN IN DAKOTA

1—The White Man's Goods 14
2—The First White Men 14
3—Seekers of the Shining Sea 16
4—The Fur Traders 17
5—Looker at Stars 18
6—Fort Pambian 19
7—Alexander Henry the Younger 19

IV—AMERICANS IN THE UPPER MISSOURI COUNTRY

1—Lewis and Clark 21
2—Boats for Big Muddy 25

3—Fur Trader Extraordinary 25
4—Finding the 49th Parallel 26
5—Getting Big White Home 26
6—The Yellowstone Expeditions 27
7—King of the Upper Missouri 27
8—Big Muddy 30
9—Fireboat upon the Water 30
10—Upper Missouri Guests 31
11-Plague upon the Prairies 32

V—RED RIVER VALLEY BEGINNINGS

1—The Selkirkers 34
2—The Pembina Hunters 34
3—Nicollet 36
4—Jolly Joe Rolette 36
5—The Red River Cartways 38
6—"St. Joe" 38
7—The Woods Expedition 39
8—Stevens Railway Survey 39
9—Fort Abercrombie 40
10—Thunder Canoes on the Red 40

VI—DAKOTA TERRITORY

1—The Beginnings 42
2—Paleface Council 44
3—The Homestead Act 44
4—Yellow Dust down Grandmother River 45
5—Misunderstanding 45

VII—WARPATH

1—The Sioux Uprising 47
2—The Siege of Fort Abercrombie 48
3—Paleface Revenge 49
4—The Sibley Expedition 49
5—Sully's Expedition of 1863 50
6—Sully's Expedition of 1864 51
7—The Goldseekers 54

VIII—DAKOTA BEGINNINGS

1—Early Struggles 56
2—Army Outposts 56
3—The First Farmer 58
4—The First Homesteaders 59
5—The Iron Trail 59
6—Bonanza Farms 60
7—Exit for Uncle Buffalo 61
8—Dakota Cowpunching 62

IX—LITTLE BIGHORN

1—The Crooked-Tongued 64
2—The Greasy Grass 66
3—Burden Bearer 68
4—Tribune Extra 69

X—DAKOTA BOOM

1—The Empire Builder 70
2—Immigrant Homesteaders 71
3—Colony Settlements 73
4—"Wrong Side Up" 74
5—Steamboat Exit 77

6—Beef Bonanza 77
7—The Great White Ruin 79
8—Badlands Dude 79
9—Old Four Eyes 81
10—A New Capital 82
11—Struggle for Statehood 83
12—Red Messiah 84

XI—THE BUILDERS

1—Flickertail State 86
2—Sodbusters and Shanty Dwellers 87
3—Around the Town Pump 89
4—Pioneer Society 92
5—Prairie Wheels 96
6—Skyways 99
7—"News Walkers" 100
8—Book Learning 102
9—Dirt Farming 107
10—The Taming of Big Muddy 111
11—From under the Good Earth 113
12—The Peace Garden State 114

Chronology 120

Index 122

Governors 124

Historic Places 124

Sources for Illustrations 126

Acknowledgements 126

1—Red River of the North

I—DAKOTA

1 - The Land

The crookedest river in the world marks the eastern border of North Dakota. This Red River runs north through some of the flattest land in the world. This flat land was once the bed of an ancient lake. That ancient Lake Agassiz formed hundreds and hundreds of years ago when a mammoth glacier melted.

Lake Agassiz covered the eastern part of what is now North Dakota. It spread out larger than all the five Great Lakes put together. Most of it reached into Canada, covering about 110,000 acres. In what we today call the Red River Valley, Lake Agassiz spread ten miles wide where Wahpeton now is and forty miles wide at Pembina. That huge lake was a hundred feet deep in the Wahpeton area and 300 feet where Grand Forks now is.

But over the centuries, Lake Agassiz became smaller and smaller as the water drained away. It left behind the fertile plain through which the lazy Red River now flows. The flat and fertile Red River Valley is about 35 miles wide within North Dakota. It slopes northward at less than one foot per mile. Where Red River of the North flows into Canada, it is 750 feet above sea level.

West of the Red River Valley, the land rises to form what we call the Drift Prairie. This gently-rolling Drift Prairie is several hundred feet higher than the Red River Valley. It includes the area around the James and Sheyenne Rivers and reaches westward beyond the Souris River. It has many small lakes, ponds, and marshes. More waterfowl hatch in North Dakota than in any other state.

Beyond the Drift Prairie we come to a jumbled belt of hills that marks the edge of the Missouri Plateau. While the Drift Prairie is from 1400 to 1600 feet above sea level, the Missouri Plateau reaches 2000 to more than 3000 feet above sea level. The muddy waters of the mighty Missouri River flowed through this part of North Dakota for centuries. Now that great dams hold back the waters of the Missouri, Lake Sakakawea and Lake Oahe have been formed. The smaller streams of the Cannonball, Heart, Knife and Little Missouri Rivers run into the Big Missouri. Along the Little Missouri we see the colorful canyons and high mesas, the

2—Ancient Lake Agassiz, larger than all the Great Lakes together (Drawing by author based on map by John P. Bluemle, geologist)

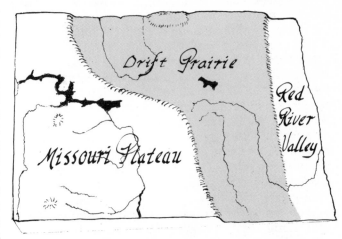

3—The three geographical regions of North Dakota (Author)

cones, domes, and buttes of the Badlands. (A butte is a tall hill with very steep sides and a flat top.) In southwestern North Dakota, White Butte reaches 3,506 feet above sea level.

We have no real mountains in North Dakota. The Turtle Mountains east of the Souris River and along the Canadian border are really hills rising high above the Drift Prairie. The Killdeer Mountains are high buttes not far from the Little Missouri River in the Missouri Plateau.

One might say that if we drive from the eastern edge of North Dakota, we travel up three "steps" as we go westward, First we have the Red River Valley, then the Drift Prairie, and thirdly, the Missouri Plateau.

From Minnesota on the east to Montana on the west, North Dakota stretches 330 miles. From South Dakota to Canada, it measures 210 miles. The state has a total area of over 70,000 square miles. North Dakota ranks 17th in size among all the states.

2 - The Prairie Primeval

The first white men to come into what is now North Dakota found it abounding in wild life. Over ninety different kinds of animals once lived here. Birds of all kinds built nests in the tall prairie grasses, in the trees along streams, and in marshes and sloughs.

Thousands of the blue-grey and red-feathered passenger pigeons made their homes in the trees along streams in the Red River Valley. Actually, this gentle bird lived in enormous flocks throughout North America, but settlers shot them or caught them with nets until today not one is alive.

Beavers made dams in the streams that flowed into Red River. These flat-tailed and sharp-toothed animals slashed entire stands of poplar or willow to build their dams and homes. Muskrats built their homes in sloughs and along streams of the Drift Prairie, many thousands of them preferring the marshlands of the Souris River area. Otters played along the Heart and Cannonball Rivers in the Missouri Plateau and the mink as well lived in great numbers along streams flowing into the Missouri River. The small weasel, reddish brown but white in winter, fed on meadow mice and moles, even sneaked into trees to kill nesting birds and devour their eggs.

Acres of wild geese and ducks flew up from Missouri River sandbars and the many sloughs and small lakes of the Drift Prairie, then strung out in soldier lines across the sky. Trumpeter swans and long-legged cranes, large-billed pelicans, and gulls nested by the millions in early-summer marshes and along lazy streams. Thousands of swallows built their nests on the steep walls of river bluffs.

In the prairie grass which often grew as high as a man's hips lived thousands upon thousands of grouse, plovers, and sage hens. Above them the golden eagle spread its great wings in flight.

Cottontail rabbits scurried about in the Red River Valley and Drift Prairie, while the long-legged jack rabbit bounded over the highlands of the Missouri Plateau. Great numbers of prairie dogs dug their underground towns on sunny, dry slopes in short-grass country. The badger sent prairie dogs scuttling into their burrows, and rattlesnakes sneaked into the prairie dog's home. The "Flicker-tails" or ground squirrels kept watchful eye for swooping owl or hawk or eagle.

In timbered glens and draws, the bobcat and lynx, the red and gray foxes, brought prey to their young. Squirrels and chipmunks and little sage rabbits raced from the larger animals that hunted them. The skunk waddled slowly about, his weapon of scent keeping most predators from him.

Pronghorn antelopes grazed the grasslands. White-tailed deer foraged from the Red River Valley and westward, while the mule deer preferred the Badlands and Little Missouri country. Elk found the Missouri bottomlands to their liking. Bighorn mountain sheep climbed the sandstone and scoria-ringed buttes and canyons of the Badlands. Moose ranged the Turtle Mountains and the Pembina hills and valleys.

In the Badlands and along the Missouri the grizzly bear roved—the only animal in all Dakota that would attack a man.

The sly coyote and the gray wolf trailed the herds of grazing animals to pounce upon one that strayed behind or was disabled.

The four-legged monarch of this prairie primeval was the buffalo. A buffalo bull could weigh as much as 2000 pounds. Of great strength, with a huge head and large humped shoulders, its short, curved horns could toss into the air or gore to death an attacking animal or hunter.

To the Indians, he was "Uncle Buffalo," for he supplied them with food, shelter, clothing, and tools. He was one of the few animals that the Indian hunted. The Indian killed only what he needed to live, for he felt a kinship with all living things sustained by their common mother—the earth. And so, when the white men first came into Dakota, they found it a hunter's paradise.

3 - Legend

In the sky-plains stretching between heaven and earth lived the Thunderbirds. When the Indian saw the lightning streak the sky, he thought the lightnings were the flashing of the Thunderbirds' fierce eyes. The Indian believed the Thunderbird wings beat the rain down from the sky. What was thunder but the cracking of Thunderbird eggs hatching?

For ages the Thunderbirds lived happily in the sky-plains. Then some looked down upon the green earth-plains of the red man. They decided it must be better to live upon the green earth. So they prayed to their Big Holy. And Big Holy let them go down to the earth. And they became giants there.

These mighty Thunderbirds could stride in one step from Grandmother River to the Shining Mountains of the Setting Sun. In another step they could reach the Great Salt Waters of the Setting Sun.

In sport one day these Thunderbird Men scooped out the basins now filled by the waters of the five Great Lakes. One Thunderbird Man with his great finger plowed a furrow from the forests of the North to the Great Waters of the South. Down that furrow did run the Mississippi, the Father of Waters.

But on earth the Thunderbird Men grew older. They longed for the sky-plains of their childhood. Again they prayed to Big Holy. And Big Holy let them shed their earth bodies and come back to the sky-plains stretching between earth and sky.

Since that ancient day, the red men saw no more Thunderbirds upon the green earth. But they saw the flashing of Thunderbird eyes in lightning. They heard the beating of Thunderbird wings bringing rain. And they knew young Thunderbirds were hatching when they heard thunder.

In the land where the Thunderbirds had once lived, the red men multiplied into tribes and nations. They roamed over the prairies, sharing Mother Earth with the animals and birds. And the buffalo, that shaggy prince of the plains, became uncle to the red man.

Proud the red man grew of his skill with feather-stick and bow. But from across the Great Salt Waters of the Rising Sun came the paleface to conquer the red man with thunderstick and firewater.

II - THE FIRST PEOPLE

1 - Indian Tribes in North Dakota

When white men began exploring what is now North Dakota, they found six different Indian tribes living here. We think the tribe that has lived here the longest was the Mandan earthlodge people who had built villages along the Missouri River.

The Hidatsa earthlodge people lived near the Mandans, and the Arikara earthlodge people moved northward to be near the other earthlodge tribes after many of their people had died from the white man's smallpox. These three tribes lived chiefly along the rivers that flowed into the Missouri from the west.

Pushed ever westward by the white man, some of the Chippewa woodland wigwam people came out of the Minnesota woods and made their homes in the wooded Pembina Hills and as far west as the Turtle Mountains.

Two tribes—the Assiniboin and the Sioux—lived on the open prairie, hunting for a living. They moved often, so they needed a lightweight dwelling they could pack and carry with them and set up quickly wherever they camped. So they made tepees covered with buffalo skins. The Assiniboin tribe stayed mostly in the northwestern part of our land and into what is now Montana and Canada, and the Sioux roamed over the southeastern part and all over what is now South Dakota.

In their hunting, however, a tribe did not stay within what it might consider its own territory. Hunting parties went wherever they found game and stayed out of hunting grounds if a stronger tribe kept them out.

2 - Uncle Buffalo

All of our prairie Indians hunted the buffalo. They spoke of this animal as "Uncle Buffalo" because they depended so much on him for food, clothing, and shelter.

From Uncle's coat came the warm robe for winter wear, for bed and covering. Tanned and scraped free of hair, Uncle's hide was made into tepee walls as well as leggings, shirts, mocassins, or a dress. Indian women stretched old, tough buffalo hides over a willow or ash frame to make a bullboat for crossing a stream. The thick skin from an old buffalo bull's neck and hump. heated over a slow fire, hardened into a shield cover that could turn a lance or arrow.

Strong sinews from Uncle Buffalo provided thread for sewing; sinews were made into bowstrings and webbing for snowshoes. Once the Indian acquired the white man's horse, he braided strips of rawhide to make lariats and tethers for his horse. Rawhide was used for saddles, bags, and drums.

Indian women used buffalo ribs as tools for dressing hides, and the shoulder blades for hoes and axes. Boiled buffalo hooves supplied glue. Softened by heat, Uncle's horns shaped into spoons and ornaments. His paunch did duty as a bucket; filled with water and with hot stones, it served as a kettle for boiling meat.

Some buffalo meat was cooked fresh, but most was dried, then pounded and mixed with berries to make into pemmican. Such dried meat would keep a long time.

The prairie Indians also hunted other grazing animals such as the deer, elk, and antelope for food and clothing, but the most desired was Uncle Buffalo.

4—Uncle Buffalo grazing in Theodore Roosevelt National Park

7—Mandan buffalo dance in which hunters urge the Great Spirit to send them buffaloes   (Catlin)

5—Buffaloes making wallows as they cover themselves with dirt or mud to protect themselves from insects (George Catlin painting)

8—Indians as wolfskin decoys hunt buffaloes with bow and arrow   (Catlin)

6—Wounded buffalo tosses unhorsed hunter   (William Carey painting)

9—Braves on snowshoes lance buffaloes caught in deep snow (Catlin)

10—The earthlodge home of the agricultural tribes (Drawing by Rebecca Jerdee)

13—Mandan village. Note bullboats in the foreground. (Bodmer)

11—Interior construction of an earthlodge (Jerdee)

14—Hidatsa winter village (Bodmer)

12—Living in an earthlodge (Karl Bodmer painting)

15—Mandan women crossing Grandmother River with their dogs and toboggans (Bodmer)

3 - The Earthlodge Farmers

Long before Columbus came to America, earthlodge women farmed in North Dakota. Their men would have nothing to do with growing crops; they did the hunting.

The earthlodge women raised beans, corn, pumpkins, sunflowers, and squash. They cultivated their small fields with buffalo shoulder blade hoes. For rakes, they tied antlers to a sturdy stick. In the center of each field, they built a sapling platform. Here girls and women sat, two or three at a time, to watch over and sing to their crops. They stored their produce in bell-shaped cellars dug under the floor of the earthlodge as well as outside.

The women built the round, dome-shaped earthlodges. Cool in summer, snug in winter, an earthlodge could give shelter to about forty persons as well as several dogs, and in severe winter storms, protected horses. (However, when the earthlodge people went on hunting trips, they used small tepees made from skins.)

Earthlodges for a family or clan ranged from thirty to ninety feet across. Lodges built for tribal councils or men's societies were large, some accommodating up to 600 people.

To construct an earthlodge with the use only of stone and flint tools was no easy job. First, the women builders usually excavated about a foot deep for the floor. They next set stout posts around the outer edge of this round floor. The posts stood about five feet above the ground. Then they laid heavy beams connecting the tops of the posts.

Toward the center of the lodge, they erected four stout logs, standing about ten feet above the ground. Heavy beams placed on the tops of these four logs formed a square frame. Only with the lifting and placing of the heavy posts and beams would the women accept help from their husbands.

They then covered this framework with smaller poles and beams. Next they laid a layer of willows or reeds, then a thatching of grass, and lastly they spread earth a foot thick over the entire earthlodge, leaving an opening in the very top. For cooking and for heat, they built a fire in a stone-lined area in the center, the smoke going out through the opening above.

The Mandan, Hidatsa, and Arikara agricultural tribes established villages of about 40 to 50 earth-lodges. The moundlike lodges huddled close together except that in the center of the village an open space gave room for dancing and tribal gatherings.

Such a village they built on a bluff or point of land jutting into a river. That way, they had protection from three sides. On the exposed side a high wall of posts and a ditch about fifteen feet wide and deep made it difficult for an enemy to attack.

Closely-knit in spirit, earthlodge people did many things together. Men and women joined in chasing buffaloes over a cliff or into a corral. They all pitched in to collect firewood.

They lived in their permanent and fortified villages most of the year. In the coldest months, they moved to smaller lodges in wooded bottom lands where fuel was plentiful, knowing their worst enemy, the Sioux, had also settled in some distant sheltered place and would stay content beside their tepee fire while snow and storm shackled the prairie land.

4 - The Tepee Travelers

The Assiniboin and Sioux women made houses suitable for travel. To set up her tepee, the wife first tied three or four poles together close to one end. She propped them up for the main tepee support, then leaned ten or more saplings against them to complete the framework.

This done, she covered the framework with a half circle of buffalo cow hides sewed together. She managed this by fastening one end of the cover to a long sapling, hoisting it to the top, next pulling the cover around and fastening it together with wooden skewers at the front.

Pegs or small rocks held the bottom edge of the cover down to keep out the wind. In hot weather the tepee cover was rolled up a few feet from the ground to let a breeze cool the tepee. Cottonwood branches laid against the sunny side helped make the tepee comfortable on a hot summer day.

For frigid temperatures the Indian wife fastened a skin lining around the inside wall of the tepee, the bottom part extending over the floor, the top reaching several feet up the wall. If desired, she stuffed grass between this lining and the wall to provide insulation against the cold. Unstuffed, it allowed an upward air current to help the smoke out the top.

After a long winter, smoke darkened the walls of the tepee. So, in the spring, when the buffaloes shed their long hair, the Indian husbands went out to hunt and get new hides for their home.

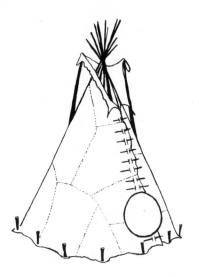

16—Buffalo-skin tepee of the plains Indians   (Jerdee)

19—A Sioux encampment. Buffalo meat is drying on racks and women are dressing skins. (Catlin)

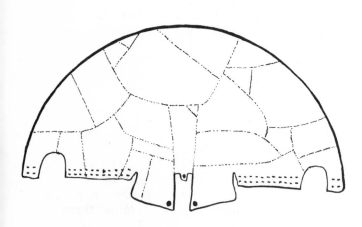

17—The tepee cover. Dotted lines indicate where skins were sewn together   (Jerdee)

20—Band of Sioux moving camp with help of travois pulled by dogs and horses   (Catlin)

18—Tepee made from 25 buffalo skins and decorated to show the accomplishments of the warrior living in it (Frank Fiske photo)

21—Sioux Indians buried their dead on scaffolds on poles or in tall trees   (David F. Barry photo)

5 - The Magic Wolf

In 1519, the Spanish explorer, Hernando Cortez, brought the first horses to the North American mainland. Some of these horses ran off and became the first of the wild horses of the West.

The Spaniards established missions and ranches in the Southwest. They raised horses, and they traded some of these horses to Indians.

The Indians learned to ride the horse and they called it the Magic Wolf or the Mystery Dog. They discovered what a wonderful help the horses were in hunting buffalo. So Indians traded horses northward from tribe to tribe.

Before they had horses, the prairie Indians depended on their dogs to help transport their tepees and other belongings from one camp to another. A dog could carry about 50 pounds on its back, or 75 pounds on a crude pole drag known as a **travois**. But a horse could carry 200 pounds on its back, or 300 pounds with a **travois**. So after an Indian tribe acquired the white man's magic wolf, they could make larger tepees. When they had only the dog to help them transport a tepee, Indian women made their houses five to six feet high; after they acquired horses, they enlarged their tepees 12 to 15 feet high.

The Indian brave became a very skillful rider, handling his horse with only a rawhide thong in its mouth. He could leap on the back of a running horse. He could hang onto one side of the horse, with only a foot over the horse's back. Hanging this way on his galloping horse, he could strike a buffalo with a spear or shoot an arrow at an enemy.

And with horses, Indians could travel farther and faster. To steal a horse from an enemy became an honor and the more horses a brave owned, the greater his tribesmen held him in respect.

6 - The Birch Bark Experts

In the northern woods, the Chippewas found a good supply of birch trees, so they used birch bark for several purposes. With birch bark they covered their dwellings and sheathed their canoes. They also used the bark for baskets and for cooking vessels. How could anyone cook in a birchbark kettle? The same way the prairie Indians used a buffalo stomach, by dropping hot stones into it.

When a Chippewa family built a wickiup or wigwam, the men cut down the saplings. One end of the saplings they set into the ground. Opposite it, they set another sapling—then lashed the tops of the two saplings together. These saplings—set in an oval shape—formed the framework of a Chippewa house.

22—Chippewa woodland wigwam   (Jerdee)

23—Interior construction of wigwam   (Jerdee)

24—Birch bark tepee   (Jerdee)

After the men had built the framework, the women spread woven mats of rushes over it. For a second covering to shed rain and snow, they used large sections of bark sewn together. For this they preferred birch bark, but if necessary, they would use elm or oak bark.

Sometimes, instead of the dome-like wigwams, the Chippewa people made birch bark tepees. To help keep the birch bark in place on both kinds of houses, they leaned logs or heavy poles against the sides.

7 - The Clan

Indians lived together more as a clan than as a family. A clan was like a permanent reunion of relatives. In some tribes, those related by blood to the mother lived together— in other tribes those related by blood to the father.

Generally, all of the clan members could not live together in one house, but whether their home was a tepee, a wigwam, or an earthlodge, the clan stayed together.

The child born in an Indian clan never lacked for attention. Not only did his own mother look after him, but his aunts were mothers to him as well, and his uncles like fathers. If he was naughty, his parents did not punish him— but his older brothers and uncles did by ridiculing him,

In some tribes an older person named the child. But when a boy reached manhood, he might earn a new name through some deed of bravery. Girls kept the same name for life.

A prairie Indian baby was carried about in a rawhide cradle. His garments were made from tender skins. The down from cattails or from cottonwood tree-pods served as diapers. At the end of the day his mother rubbed his body in buffalo tallow, and as he grew she exposed his body more and more to the air so that he could become "face all over."

The women of a lodge trained a girl in the skills she must know as a wife and mother. Girls joined with women in picking berries and swimming. Earthlodge girls took turns with their mothers in caring for the fields and singing to the corn.

A boy learned early to shoot arrows of slough grass with a tiny twig arrow. Handling a bow and arrow became as natural as running and jumping. Small boys followed older boys on rabbit hunts, and when they killed a rabbit they decorated their hair with his tail.

An Indian boy looked forward to the time when he could hunt and go on the warpath so that he could prove his worth. Always, when he played, he imagined an enemy lurked nearby. Thus he developed a constant alertness to his surroundings.

When an Indian mother gave food to a weak or old member of the band or clan, she had her child carry some of the food so he could learn to share in the giving. Indians prized generosity as one of the greatest of virtues. An honored brave was one who could give away prized possessions.

The Indian child learned that not only did food nourish his body, but so did the sun, the air, and water. For this reason, he wore as little clothing as possible, and bathed as often as he could.

When an Indian boy grew up, he could not consider getting married until he had proved himself as a warrior and a hunter. He must show that he could protect and provide for his wife and children. Likewise, a girl must learn all the skills she would need in caring for her husband, her children, and her lodge before she would be considered ready to marry.

Customs varied, but generally when a young brave had found the girl he wanted for his wife, his family would bring important gifts to the girl's family. If the girl's family— usually her father— considered the gifts worthy of the girl, this was the same as agreeing to the marriage. In some tribes the bride's family would then give presents—and a feast—to the young brave's family. If it was an earthlodge family, the young man came to live with the bride's family and he became part of her clan. Among other tribes, the girl would go to live with her husband's clan.

The Indian husband hunted the animals from which his wife got meat and skins. He helped protect his tribe from an enemy. He revenged those of his tribe or clan that had been harmed. His tribe praised him for stealing horses from an enemy tribe, but scorned him if he stole anything from a fellow tribesman.

When his family followed a trail, the husband walked ahead of his wife and children to protect them from any startled animal or enemy. So that he could be free to protect, he carried only his weapons while his wife had the responsibility of transporting family goods. The heavier of such goods the wife laid on a **travois** pulled by a dog or a horse.

The good wife skinned, cleaned, and tanned the hides of animals which her husband supplied her. From these she sewed with bone needle and sinew the clothing, bags, and tepee coverings needed. She gathered berries, wild turnips and peas. The earthlodge wife also tended her field and made pottery. In her spare time, she embroidered with porcupine quills and elk's teeth.

If her husband brought a guest home to her lodge, the wife fed them both and repaired the guest's torn clothing or gave him new. To give to others gave both husband and wife satisfaction. It also showed that the husband was a good provider who kept his lodge well supplied.

25—On the left side: woodland moccasin, Chippewa man's apron, and Chippewa woman's dress with tie-on sleeves. On the right: hard-soled plains moccasin, plains breech cloth, and plains woman's yoke dress   (Jerdee)

8 - What the Indian Gave Us

Our American way of life is blessed by many gifts from the American Indian.

Plants grown first by Indians furnish much food now eaten by people not only in America but in other parts of the world. We eat many Indian foods such as corn, white potatoes, avocados, kidney and lima beans, pumpkins, squash, sweet potatoes, sunflowers, tomatoes, peppers, cashew nuts, peanuts, pineapples and wild rice. Indians taught us about chewing gum and how to get sugar and syrup from maple trees. (The earthlodge Indians also used the sap from boxelder trees.) Indians showed us how to make corn pone, succotash, hominy, and other native foods. Early traders and settlers made much use of Indian pemmican.

We wear cotton clothes. Indians grew cotton in the southern part of our country long before white men came here. The long fiber cotton now being grown in Africa came from that grown by American Indians. We wear Indian moccasins.

At the drugstore we can buy the Indian's oil of wintergreen, his arnica, and witch hazel. Many modern medicines come from the herbs Indians used.

Indians gave us popcorn. They taught us to plant corn in hills, and to grow pumpkins and squash in cornfields.

Few of us realize the richness of many Indian languages. The Sioux Indians spoke in a language that numbered over 19,000 words. (The ancient Hebrew language in which the Old Testament was written had only a 10,000-word vocabulary.) More than five hundred Indian words have become part of our English language. Some of these words common to North Dakotans are **coyote, skunk, moose, toboggan, wigwam, tepee,** and **caucus.**

Nearly half of our states have Indian names. In North Dakota we have towns with Indian names (Absaraka, Lakota, Makoti, Mandan, Menoken, Michigan, Minnewaukan, Niagara, Omemee, Pembina, Tioga, Wahpeton); rivers (Missouri, Sheyenne; and lakes (Metigoshe, Oahe, Sakakawea, Tewaukan).

In our recreation and sports, we play lacrosse, one of the favorite games of Indians. We go canoeing, tobogganing, and snowshoeing because the Indians showed us how.. We relax in hammocks invented by Indians. Out in the woods, we can call a moose the way Indians taught us..

Boy Scouts and campers have used much Indian wood lore. They have made Indian clothes and learned Indian dances. Sibley army tents were copied after Indian tepees. Both young and old enjoy Indian handicrafts as hobbies.

We do bead and shell jewelry and embroidery in Indian designs. Women carry handbags beaded in Indian styles; we wear belts and headbands of Indian patterns.

Indian figures have appeared on our money. The Indian- head penny was first minted in 1859. The Indian-head nickel first minted in 1913 was modeled after two Midwest Indians: Iron Tail, a Sioux who took part in Buffalo Bill's Wild West Shows, and Two Moons, a Cheyenne chief who helped defeat Custer in 1876.

26—The Chippewa people made designs based on leaf and flower forms. (Jerdee)

27—Hidatsa maiden   (Catlin)

28—Imogene Baker, Concordia College homecoming queen, 1938, wearing Mandan ceremonial garb of her family

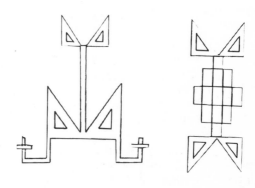

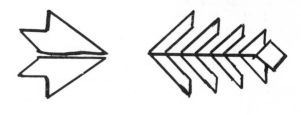

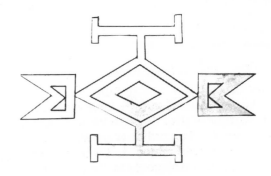

29—Plains Indian geometric designs   (Jerdee)

Story of the Peace Garden State, page 13

III - THE FIRST WHITE MEN IN DAKOTA

1 - The White Man's Goods

Before they ever saw a white man, some of the prairie Indians had traded for his glass beads, steel knives and hatchets, metal needles, his gun, and most prized of all—his horse. How could this come about?

Neighboring tribes traded goods with one another. Even enemy tribes would declare a truce long enough so that they could barter. The earthlodge people traded their corn and vegetables to the plains hunters for meat and skins as well as sea shells. The shells had been traded, tribe by tribe, from as far away as the Gulf of Mexico. Likewise, the horse was traded up from the southwest where the Spaniards had first settled.

Eastern tribes traded with the white men. Then these tribes traded the white man's goods with neighbor tribes further west. Thus when white men first came into our prairie land, they found Indians outfitted with products from Europe.

Every tribe had its own language. Even the Mandan, Arikara, and Hidatsa who lived together each had their separate language. Yet they would trade with the Sioux, the Assiniboin, the Chippewa, the Crows from the Montana area or Crees from up in the Canadian territory.

How? They used a sign language which was much the same among tribes all over America. For hours at a time, men from different tribes would "talk" with their hands. They not only did this in order to trade goods, but also to exchange news or information.

2 - The First White Men

We can never know the name of the first white man to step onto North Dakota ground.

In Europe at that time, kings and emperors ruled the countries. The ordinary person was considered inferior and was subject not only to the king, but also to upper class people known as nobles. Nobles lived in castles and great manor houses and ruled over parts of a country in the place of their king. The king and the nobles owned the land, but the ordinary people (known as peasants) did all the labor.

After Columbus had discovered America and claimed the land for his Spanish king, other European kings sent explorers to America to claim for themselves territories in the new land. In 1610, Henry Hudson, exploring for the English, sailed into Hudson's Bay and claimed for England all the land drained by rivers running into Hudson's Bay. Thus the land through which our Red River flows was considered the property of the English. Earlier, the French had explored and claimed the north Atlantic coastlands for France, and they called this territory New France.

In 1608, the French explorer, Samuel de Champlain, founded a settlement on the St. Lawrence River. It would become the first city in what is now Canada. Champlain named the settlement Quebec, an Indian word which means "the place where the river narrows." Many years later, another French explorer, Robert de la Salle, sailed across the Great Lakes. Then he went down the Illinois River to the mouth of the Missouri River and claimed all the land drained by these rivers for his king, Louis XIV of France.

The beaver hat and the furs of mink, marten, and fox became fashionable to wear at the courts of kings and nobles, and so the demand for furs from American colonies increased greatly.

At Quebec, French peasants were sent out to trap beavers, mink, marten, and fox—and to barter with Indians for such. The Indians prized the bright glass beads, the glittering trinkets, the red cloth, and white man's weapons and willingly traded furs which would sell at high prices in Europe.

The King of France ordered that the governor at Quebec should require all fur traders to pay for a license before they would be allowed to go into the wilderness for furs.

Out in the wilderness the French peasants found freedom and adventure. A man could do as he pleased, bowing to no master. The King of France and the governor of Quebec could not reach them in the wilderness. And so hundreds of Frenchmen, refusing to buy a license, escaped from those who would rule over them.

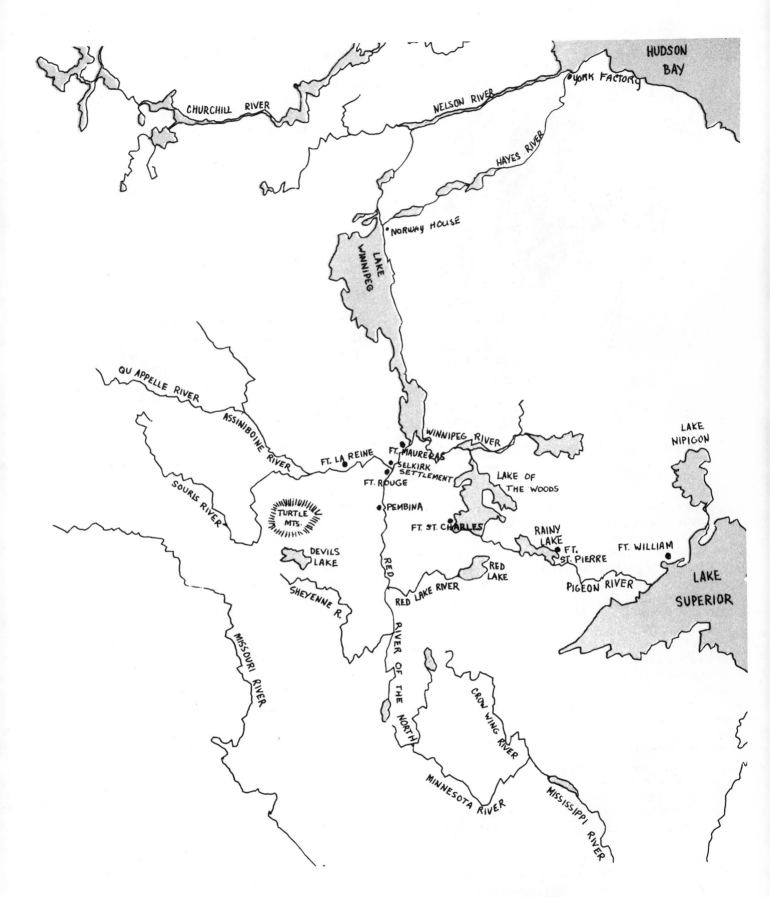

30—Map showing the "Up Country" through which the first white men (the earliest fur traders, the Verendryes, and David Thompson) came into the North Dakota area. (Map by Don Opsal)

Story of the Peace Garden State, page 15

31—Painting of typical early fur trader or trapper (S. Paxson)

The voyageur provided the labor for transporting trade goods and furs. Voyageurs were seldom tall because a long-legged man took too much room in a crowded canoe. The sturdy voyageur paddled as many as eighteen hours a day. When American rebels were fighting for independence, it is estimated that there were 2500 voyageurs working for traders and trading companies in the Great Lakes area.

So it is quite likely that the first white man to come into what is now North Dakota was a Frenchman seeking beaver pelts in the Red River Valley where beavers lived in great numbers.

3 - Seekers of the Shining Sea

The first recorded visit of a white man to what is now North Dakota took place when George Washington was six years old and Daniel Boone had not yet crossed the Alleghenies into Kentucky.

When Pierre de la Verendrye commanded the Lake Nipigon trading post north of Lake Superior, he learned from the Indians that a tribe of Indians lived on a westward flowing river. On this river, they said, one could paddle to the Shining Mountains and beyond the Shining Mountains go to the great salt waters.

Verendrye wanted to find those Shining Mountains and the Shining Sea beyond. The governor of New France gave him permission to go exploring, but Verendrye would have to pay his own expenses. Having no money himself, Verendrye convinced merchants at Montreal to provide him needed supplies with the understanding that he would send back furs to keep accounts balanced.

So on June 8, 1731, Verendrye and fifty men paddled supply-laden canoes westward from Montreal. With Verendrye went his three sons, Jean, Pierre, and Francois.

For seven hard years, Verendrye struggled slowly westward. Several times a party of his men would have to return to Montreal for supplies. At one time his men mutinied when they had to live on boiled roots and strips of moccasin leather. Indians killed his eldest son, Jean.

Verendrye established several small trading posts in what is now Minnesota and Canada. While he was exploring the area about the Assiniboine and Souris Rivers, the Assiniboin Indians told him that the earthlodge people would know the way to the great salt waters beyond the Shining Mountains.

Verendrye headed for the Mandan earthlodge villages, and as he traveled, about six hundred Assiniboins joined him. The Mandan people welcomed Verendrye and treated him hospitably. But

They made friends with the Indians, learned to live with the Indians and to speak their language. They trapped beaver and traded with Indians for furs. After a year of hunting and trading, they packed their pelts into bundles, and the bundles into their birch-bark canoes. They joined other Frenchmen and headed for Quebec to trade their furs for more goods to barter with their Indian friends.

As this fur trade increased, trading posts were established along the Great Lakes, small ones first by a trader, then larger ones by fur trade companies.

A company trading post was built near water and wood supply, convenient to the Indians. A square or rectangular stockade up to twenty feet high enclosed grounds for the storehouse and office, shops, and dwellings for post employees. In the center of the enclosure rose a flag staff. A cannon near the staff base pointed toward the one gate entrance. Two blockhouses on diagonally opposite corners of the stockade defended the four walls of the fort from attack

Boss of the trading post was the bourgeois (French) or factor (English). In a wilderness having no police, sheriff, judge, or jury, his word was law for the hunters, trappers, blacksmith, carpenter, boatbuilder, and **voyageurs** employed by the post.

32—Statue of Pierre de la Verendrye

one Mandan chief, considering how many baskets of corn and squash the uninvited Assiniboins would eat, told them that the dread Sioux were on their way to attack. Frightened by this, the Assiniboins quickly retreated to their northern hunting grounds.

Verendrye soon learned that the Mandans had never seen the great western sea and could not tell him how to get there. Then, through blizzards and storms, he returned to his nearest post. Weary and sick, he later returned to Montreal.

For two years (1742-1743) Francois and Louis de la Verendrye continued their father's search. Just what territories the Verendrye brothers explored is not known for sure. They may have gone as far west as the Big Horn Mountains or the Black Hills. A plaque which they buried on March 30, 1743, was found by schoolchildren near Pierre, South Dakota, 170 years later.

After thirteen years of searching, the Verendryes failed to find the Shining Mountains and the ocean beyond. But they learned that the "westward-flowing river" was really the Missouri which flowed south to join the Mississippi.

Pierre de la Verendrye, at the age of 64, prepared to try again, but even as he made ready, he died.

The Verendryes were the first white men to discover and explore the Saskatchewan, Assiniboine, Red and upper Missouri rivers, and to explore into what is now North Dakota, South Dakota, Wyoming, and Montana.

4 - The Fur Traders

In the early years of our country, several thousand men may have been trapping and trading furs in the vast wilderness west and north of the Great Lakes. Some doubtless roamed the North Dakota area. Few of these men could read and write, and those who could write were not interested in leaving a record of their adventures and wanderings.

A law unto themselves, they lived alone or in Indian villages. They learned to talk less and less in a wilderness where silence protected one's life and helped the hunter stalk the wild beast. Tanned from living constantly in the open, wearing the buckskin leggings and shirts of the Indian, these white brothers to the red men became like Indians in their appearance and ways.

They carried no money, for money had no value in the wilderness. So they bartered with the Indians in order to get furs from them. In the early years of fur trade, the beaver served as the unit of exchange. For example, for 12 beaver skins the white man would give one gun to the Indian; four pelts exchanged for a pistol; for one beaver skin the Indian could get half a pound of glass beads, an iron kettle or a pound of tobacco. The number of beaver skins required in trade would change over the years, depending on the circumstance.

These woodsmen cared little about what happened in the countries they had left behind. It mattered not to a Frenchman if he trapped in territory claimed by the English, nor did it matter to an Englishman or a Scotsman if he traded in French territory. But news doubtless reached them that England and France went to war. In America, it was the French and Indian War fought from 1754 to 1763 and in Europe it was called the Seven Years' War.

A year before the English captured Quebec, France ceded her Mississippi River territory to Spain. When the British won the French and Indian War, France was left with no land in America. Thus the prairies of North Dakota were divided between Spain and England, Spain claiming that drained by the Missouri, England the watershed of the Souris and the Red.

In 1764 the St. Louis trading post was established on the west side of the Mississippi River just a few miles below the mouth of the Missouri River. Thirty miles upstream the Illinois River furnished a route to the Great Lakes.

The first man to row up the Missouri to the Mandan villages was a Frenchman, Jacques D'Eglise. He reached the earthlodge people in 1792. He found two Frenchmen, Menard and Jusseasume, living there with the Indians. D'Eglise also learned that a Scotsman, James McKay, had also visited the Mandans a year before Menard had come there.

33—Voyageurs on way to fur trade station. (Frances Anne Hopkins painting)

McKay later went down to St. Louis and in August, 1795, he set out with an expedition of thirty-three men to establish fur-trade posts on the Platte River. The following year McKay sent a Welshman, John Evans, to go up the Missouri to the Mandans. Evans reached the Mandans on September 23, 1796. He distributed medals, flags, and other presents and urged the earthlodge people to trade with the Spanish who now claimed all the land drained by the Mississippi and its tributaries.

Up at Hudson Bay, the fur-trading Hudson's Bay Company established its first forts. Chartered by the King of England, this company claimed full right to hunting and trading in the vast region where rivers drained into Hudson Bay. But Scottish storekeepers in Quebec organized another company, the North West Fur Company to trade into the Red River Valley area—and fierce competition began between the two companies.

So as the fur traders began to compete for trade with the Indians, hostile feelings developed between the different fur-trading companies. And the friendly and respectful spirit in which the white traders first dealt with the Indians became more and more harsh and demanding.

5 - Looker at Stars

A gentle young man, David Thompson, came to York, a post on the shore of Hudson Bay. There he hired as bookkeeper for the Hudson's Bay Company. From the surveyor employed by the Company, young David learned how to survey. He then explored and surveyed for the Company for thirteen years, traveling over 9000 miles in the wilderness.

In May, 1797, David quit working for the Hudson's Bay Company and journeyed to Grand Portage on Lake Superior. There he hired as a surveyor for the North West Company. The Scottish owners of the Company wanted him to find if any of their fur trade posts were south of the 49th parallel, in U. S. territory. They also wanted him to find the source of the Mississippi as well as to visit the Mandan Indians.

David Thompson then made his way back to McDonnel's House (about 20 miles southeast of what is now Brandon, Manitoba) on the Souris River. There he organized an expedition to the Mandan earthlodge villages. Leaving the post on November 28, the party traveled for 238 miles in sub- zero weather, often in blizzards, and depending for most of their food on wild game hunted along the way. For shelter and fuel, they camped in wooded places. Their route took them along the southwest loop of the Souris River, past the Turtle Mountains, then out across the prairies toward the Missouri. They celebrated Christmas Eve at Dog Den Butte.

The first Indians they came upon lived in an unfortified Hidatsa winter village. From here they continued to other villages of the Mandan and Hidatsa, enjoying two weeks of earthlodge hospitality. The traders bartered for wolf and fox furs, while Thompson worked on the first map ever made in North Dakota.

Then with thirty-one dogs hitched to their sleds, the party struck back through storms and bitter cold. They reached McDonnel House on February 3, 1798.

Thompson did not rest long before he set out again for the Red River. He found Fort Pambian which Charles Chaboillez had established for the North West Company. Thompson's surveying showed that the fort was in United States territory, so he advised Chaboillez to move it further north.

The following summer David Thompson married the daughter of an Irish trader. For a number of years he explored the Pacific Northwest and established trading posts. In 1812 he joined the annual brigade of canoes bound for Montreal and never returned to the Up Country over which he had tramped and explored for 23 years.

David Thompson died in poverty at Montreal. No stone was placed to mark the grave of this man who today is considered the most renowned geographer of the New World.

At Verendrye, North Dakota, the Great Northern Railway Company erected the David Thompson Memorial. On the base of this monument we read: "1770—David Thompson—1857. Geographer and astronomer passed near here in 1797 and 1798 on a scientific and trading expedition. He made the first map of the country which is now North Dakota and achieved many noteworthy discoveries in the northwest."

34—Thompson memorial, Verendrye, North Dakota

35—Red River Carts arriving at Pembina fur post

6 - Fort Pambian

First post in North Dakota at which a journal was kept was that of Charles Chaboillez's North West trading post established at the junction of the Pembina and Red River in September, 1797. (It is possible that a trading post existed at this place as early as 1780.)

Charles Chaboillez, at 55 a veteran of the fur trade, set out with a brigade of canoes from Grand Portage on Lake Superior, August 5, 1797. For 48 days he led his men over the northern canoe route which would become a much-used highway for transporting goods and furs. After leaving Lake Superior, this route went by way of Rainy Lake, Lake of the Woods, the Winnipeg River, Winnipeg Lake, then south up the Red River. Chaboillez's four large canoes carried heavy loads of gunpowder and shot, tobacco, kettles, beaver traps, blankets, beads, ornaments, firesteels and gunflints. And he brought a good supply of rum. He diluted the rum with two parts of water. Then, like other traders, Chaboillez gave this diluted rum to Indians to drink, for when an Indian had become drunk, he would barter his furs for ridiculously little in return.

When he had begun building his trading post, Chaboillez learned that a man from the Hudson's Bay Company was also building a trading post a mile and a half to the south. Rivalry between the two posts became fierce so that the Indians were treated with much rum at both places.

In March, David Thompson arrived, surveyed, and found Fort Pambian just inside United States territory. The next month the Red River flooded. Water crested over the stockade after all the goods had been moved to high ground. In May, Chaboillez stowed 48 packs of furs into his canoes and headed for Grand Portage and very likely never returned.

7 - Alexander Henry the Younger

Alexander Henry, the Canadian trapper, gained much fame for his travels and explorations from Montreal to the Rocky Mountains. Not as well known was his nephew of the same name who traded for furs in the Red River Valley.

The North West Company sent this nephew, known as Henry the Younger, to establish trading posts along the Red River in 1800. With eight heavily-laden canoes, he and his men left Grand Portage on July 19, and followed the fur trade route of connecting lakes and streams leading northwest to Lake Winnipeg. Here, in August, he turned his expedition south up the Red River. Along the way, he outfitted men to set up stations on the Roseau River and in the Pembina Hills.

Henry's party passed deserted Fort Pambian and on September 8 camped on Park River. The men now chopped oak logs for a storehouse in which Henry deposited his trade goods under a grass-and-earth roof. Fearful of Sioux attack, the men worked fast to build a stockade of 15-foot timbers. When they completed the post on October 18, Henry raised the British flag. That same day neighboring Indians brought in 40 bears they had killed and Indians and whites celebrated together.

A tall oak tree served Henry as a look-out tower from which he could spy over the land and see the great abundance of game. During that winter at Park River, he collected the skins of 643 beavers, 125 black bears, 23 brown bears, 2 grizzly bears, 83 wolves, 102 red foxes, 178 fishers, 96 otters, 26 martens, and 63 minks besides various other pelts and many bags of pemmican, bales of meat, and bags of grease.

Henry's men traded with the Indians wherever they found their encampments. For fear of the Sioux, Henry's Indian guides would never take him beyond the present location of Caledonia. The abundance of game led to waste, for often only the tongue and choice cuts of the buffalo were taken.

In the spring, rising flood waters forced Henry out of his Park River fort and he moved to the site at Pembina. Before he began building, he planted a garden, then set out for Grand Portage to complete a year's profitable business.

Henry completed his Fort Pembina where Chaboillez had first built his Fort Pambian. But now he found himself close to his competitors—a Hudson's Bay Company post and a post built by a new company, known as the XY.

In his regularly-kept journal, Henry wrote on November 15, 1801: "Men now go again for meat, with small carts, the wheels of which are each of one solid piece, sawed off the ends of trees, whose diameter is three feet. These carriages we find much more convenient and advantageous than it is to load horses, the country being so smooth and level that we can use them in every direction." These carts were the earliest forms of the famous Red River Carts which, half a century later, would carry freight from Pembina to St. Paul, Minnesota.

Two years later, this first white gardener in North Dakota, reported happily: "Snow. I took my vegetables up— 300 large heads of cabbages, 8 bushels of carrots, 16 bushels of onions, 10 bushels of turnips, some beets, parsnips, etc." Three days later, he wrote: "I took in my potatoes, 420 bushels, the produce of 7 bushels.... I measured an onion, 22 inches in diameter; a carrot, 18 inches long and, at the thick end, 14 inches in circumference; a turnip with its leaves weighed 25 pounds and the leaves alone weighed 15 pounds. The common weight is from 9 to 12 pounds, without the leaves."

Henry the Younger started the first poultry flock in North Dakota when he brought a rooster and two hens to his Pembina post in 1807.

He wrote that "mice destroy everything. They eat my pelts and skins." Wood ticks and mosquitoes plagued him. Then when grasshoppers destroyed his gardens and stripped the trees of leaves, Henry deserted Fort Pembina and went to a post in northwestern Canada.

IV - Americans in the Upper Missouri Country

1 - Lewis and Clark

President Thomas Jefferson believed that for the United States to keep its independence, the country must reach from the Atlantic to the Pacific. The British claimed the Canadian territories from the East coast to the West. Spain had returned the territory drained by the Mississippi to France and it was named the Louisiana Territory. Russia had established herself in Alaska. The Spaniards in California roved further and further up the Pacific Coast. But no country had yet laid claim to the Pacific Northwest.

So Jefferson obtained permission from the French for an American expedition to cross the Louisiana Territory so that Americans could explore into the Pacific Northwest. At this time, France was badly in need of money. So in 1803, before such an expedition started out, France sold the Louisiana Territory to the United States for fifteen million dollars or three cents an acre. (The Louisiana Territory was so large that thirteen states, in whole or in part, developed out of the area.)

Now the expedition must not be delayed to go beyond the Shining Mountains and go down the river the Indians said flowed westward into the Great Waters. America must be the first to raise her flag there!

President Jefferson selected his secretary, Meriweather Lewis to head the Expedition. Lewis insisted that his friend, Captain William Clark, go with him to share the responsibilities. The Expedition had three purposes: to find a trade route to the Pacific, to make friends with Indian tribes along the way, and plant the American flag in the Oregon wilderness.

The Lewis and Clark Expedition included nine Kentucky frontiersmen, 14 soldiers, two Frenchmen to serve as interpreter and hunter, and York, Clark's black servant. Because of danger from the Sioux, an escort of nine boatmen, six privates and a corporal in charge, would go with the Expedition as far as the Mandan villages.

The Expedition went up the Missouri River in a 55-foot keelboat equipped with a sail and 22 oars. A narrow, cleated catwalk on either side of the

36—Captain William Clark

37—Captain Meriweather Lewis

38—"Keelboat on the Missouri," drawing by Paul Rockwood

keelboat gave footing for pushing the boat with poles. Or the boat could be pulled by rope by men on shore. They also had two boats fastened together by a connecting platform.

These boats carried a heavy load for gifts and trade with the Indians: bales containing 500 fancy bracelets, 15 dozen small mirrors, 4600 needles, 70 yards of red cloth, coats bright with gilt braid, red trousers, colored handkerchiefs, glass beads, medals, and flags. For the men themselves the boats transported guns and ammunition, clothes, and limited food rations because much of their food must come from hunting and trade with the farmer Indians.

When they reached the Arikara earthlodge villages at the mouth of the Grand River, they found this tribe ready to go on the warpath against the Mandans. The white captains told the Arikaras that this was foolish. The Mandans and Arikaras were small nations, were they not? Did it not make more sense for them to unite against their common enemy, the Sioux? The Arikara said they would open their ears to such white man's counsel. And their Chief Arketarnashar agreed to travel with the white men to the Mandan villages and there smoke the peace pipe.

On the cold and wet morning of Sunday, October 14, 1804, the 45 men halted their three boats on a Missouri River sandbar and ate. They had reached what is now North Dakota.

Along the way they now met a couple French fur traders, and two North West Company traders from Fort Assiniboine in Canada. And they saw large numbers of buffalo, elk, and deer as well as some grizzly bears.

On October 26 Clark took the Arikara chief ashore to meet the Mandan chiefs. The white captains gave the head chiefs of each village an American flag, a medal of President Jefferson, a coat with gilt braid, a hat and a feather. The lesser chiefs received other tokens of good will. And the chiefs smoked the calumet with Chief Arketarnashar. After that the council came to an end with the firing of the little cannon on the keelboat.

The captains selected a site for their winter fort on the east side of the Missouri about four miles from the Mandan villages. The white men began construction on November 3 and never lacked for Indian onlookers. They completed the three-sided fort on December 24. They raised the American flag (then having 17 stars) for the first time in North Dakota on Christmas Day, 1804.

Two shots from the little swivel cannon and a round of small arms welcomed the New Year at Fort Mandan. Sixteen of the men visited the earthlodge villages, the Frenchman, Cruzat. bringing along his fiddle. The white men danced for the villagers. Cruzat delighted them with dancing on his hands.

Because of his red hair, the Indians called Clark Chief Redhead. But York, the black man, fascinated them. He enjoyed showing off his great strength. When an Hidatsa chief first saw York, he wet his fingers and rubbed the black man's skin to make sure York was not "a white man painted black."

The Expedition blacksmith set up his forge, and here North Dakota lignite was used for the first time. Through the winter, the Indians brought gifts of corn and vegetables for the axes, knives, and iron arrowpoints the blacksmith made or sharpened for them.

Lewis and Clark hired three Frenchmen as interpreters: John LePage for the Cheyennes, Rene Jusseaume for the Mandans, and Toussaint Charbonneau for the Hidatsa. These interpreters brought their Indian wives to live with them at Fort Mandan. Among these was the youngest of Charbonneau's three wives—a Shoshone girl that had been captured by the Hidatsas. She had been named Sakakawea, an Hidatsa word meaning Bird Woman.

Gentle Sakakawea tried eagerly to please the white men. She wanted to see her own people again and told the two captains she remembered the way back to the mountains of her Shoshone tribe. She could help the white men get horses from the Shoshone.

On February 11, 1805, Sakakawea gave birth to a boy, and Lewis and Clark questioned whether they should bring the young mother along on the westward explorations.

Wanting lighter boats for the journey west, the Expedition men that winter made six dugout canoes. Then in the spring they readied the keelboat for its return to St. Louis. On it they stored specimens of plants, the skins of various animals, some stuffed specimens as well as a few live birds and animals in cages, and some Indian gifts—all addressed to the President of the United States.

On Sunday, April 7, 1805, the Arikara chief, Brave Raven and three warriors came to Fort Mandan to ask that the white captains ask the Assiniboins to be at peace with the Arikara. And, said Brave Raven, the Arikara would now come to live near the Mandan and Hidatsa people.

That same afternoon, the keelboat with the returning soldiers aboard started down the Missouri for St. Louis. In the opposite direction the Expedition men set out in the heavily-loaded dugouts, thirty-three persons in all. And Sakakawea, her little baby in a cradleboard upon her back, looked forward to seeing her own people again.

On April 26, after passing the mouth of the Yellowstone River, they camped for the night on the north bank of the Missouri, approximately at the present Montana-North Dakota line. That evening Clark wrote in his journal that the place would make an excellent location for a fort. (Within a quarter of a century, one of the most famous American fur posts, Fort Union, was established there.)

The Expedition met no hostile Indians, but they did meet up with hostile grizzly bears. At one time, a wounded grizzly lunged after the hunters who then leaped from a 20-foot high embankment into the Missouri. The bear leaped after them, snapping at the heels of the hindmost swimmer until a bullet

39—Lewis and Clark arriving at a Mandan village (R. W. Smith painting)

40—Model of Fort Mandan

41—Grizzly bear hunt (Bodmer)

42—Statue of Sakakawea on the capitol grounds, Bismarck (Leonard Crunelle, sculptor)

shot from shore finished the grizzly. Rattlesnakes and prickly pears also kept men on shore alert.

Sakakawea, her baby on her back, found sunflower seeds, artichokes, roots, and berries for the men to eat. She warned against water unfit to drink, gathered herbs with which to treat the sick and made ointments to put on sores and insect bites.

On August 17 they met the Shoshones. And great was Sakakawea's joy to discover the chief was her brother, Cameahwait. She gave him a lump of sugar and encouraged him to be friends with the white men. Then she coaxed him to trade horses to Lewis and Clark and to furnish a guide across the Mountains of Bright Stones to the headwaters of the river that flowed westward to the Great Waters.

Beyond the Bitter Root Mountains, the Expedition left their horses with the Nez Perce Indians, then went down the Clearwater River in dugout canoes. They built their winter fort near where Astoria, Oregon, now is.

In late March, 1806 the party started back for the United States. After crossing the Rocky Mountains, they split at Lolo Pass. Lewis took a northern route through Lewis Pass, thence down the Missouri. Clark followed the route they had already traveled to Three Forks, then across country to the Yellowstone River. The two parties planned to meet where the Yellowstone flows into the Missouri.

Captain Clark's party reached the North Dakota meeting place August 3. Here mosquitoes tormented them so badly they could not sleep, and the next morning—after leaving a note for Lewis on a tree—they continued down river. Several days later, rid of the mosquitoes, they met four hunters in bullboats. Indians had stolen the hunters' horses so they had made the bullboats so they could get on their way.

Three days later, Clark's party met two other white men on their way to hunt along the Yellowstone River.

Meanwhile, eight Blackfeet warriors tried stealing horses from the Lewis party. The Indians did not succeed and the whites killed two of them in the skirmish that followed. Then they mounted their horses and raced for their lives from any Blackfeet that might pursue them.

They caught up with Clark's party at a point about five miles below the present day Four Bears Bridge.

On August 14 the Expedition reached the Hidatsa and Mandan villages on Knife River. They just missed meeting Henry the Younger who had come there from Pembina to trade. A prairie fire had burned Fort Mandan to the ground, but warm welcome awaited the white men in the earthlodges.

Lewis and Clark held council with the chiefs and invited them to come along and visit the Great White Father at Washington. But the chiefs covered their ears to such an invitation, for they feared the Sioux further down the Missouri.

Young John Colter asked the captains to release him from the Expedition so that he could join the hunters heading for the Yellowstone. Colter had given excellent service and was no longer needed, so the Captains said he could go.

The Expedition captains paid Charbonneau $500 for his services. Sakakawea who had been so helpful to the Expedition expected no pay, and received none.

Big White, the Mandan chief, agreed to go with the captains to visit the Great White Father. With him went his wife, Yellow Corn, and their small son, White-Painted Horse.

Three days later, on August 20, the Lewis and Clark Expedition left the North Dakota area. They reached Washington in February, 1807, after more than two years and four months in the wilderness. Lewis was then appointed governor of the Louisiana Territory, and Clark was made brigadier-general of the Territory's militia.

The Lewis and Clark Expedition explorations gave the United States claim to the Oregon territory. So the United States now stretched from the Atlantic to the Pacific.

The expedition brought back accounts and specimens of animals so far unknown to Americans: the grizzly bear, silver fox, antelope, prairie dog, mountain goat, bighorn sheep and such birds as white cranes and several species of ducks and geese.

43—Mackinaw boat such as used for floating down the Missouri River. This photo shows a party of men, women, and children leaving Fort Benton, Montana, in 1878.

2 - Boats for Big Muddy

With the return of the Lewis and Clark Expedition, attention turned more and more to the Northwest. Hundreds, then thousands, of white men would soon travel the Big Muddy beyond the Mandans—first for furs, then for gold, and finally to seek homes.

Different river boats served these travelers. A man going by himself or a companion or two hewed a dugout canoe out of a cottonwood tree. Two such boats they sometimes fastened together with a connecting platform to provide extra load space. Known as pirogues, these had a sail, but were also pulled from shore, or moved with oars.

Independent fur traders floated up to six thousand pounds of furs in a bullboat such as the earthlodge people had made. But when a company of men organized to trade, the sturdy keelboat such as Lewis and Clark had used served best.

A keelboat might be 75 feet long. Cargo filled up most of the boat. A favorable wind could push the sail-equipped keelboat as much as 70 miles in a day. With no wind, the men rowed, or they pulled the boat from the shore. The Missouri proved a treacherous stream because the bedstream constantly shifted, and bluffs and banks occasionally caved in. To pull a keelboat sometimes meant slogging through mud or trudging hip deep in water. Usually, it took about four times as long to travel up the Big Muddy as to come down it.

For transporting goods downstream, the mackinaw supplied the cheapest way. A flat-bottomed boat usually pointed at both ends, it measured up to 40 and 50 feet long. A crew of five men guided it seventy to a hundred miles a day. When the mackinaw reached its destination, it was taken apart and the lumber used for building.

Life in the Upper Missouri country often proved brutal. Among well-meaning tradesmen, there came also criminals who had escaped from the law. Where there was no established law, each man was a law unto himself. Lewis and Clark had exchanged gifts with the Indians and had known the

hospitality of the earthlodge people. But as greed for furs increased, the trader took advantage of the Indian and so many an Indian came to look upon the white man as his enemy. And white men traveling the Big Muddy frequently lost their lives to Indian attack from the shore.

44—Manuel Lisa

3 - Fur Trader Extraordinary

Up the Missouri in a keelboat came Manuel Lisa the first spring after Lewis and Clark had returned to Washington. Forty-two men he had with him, sixteen thousand dollars' worth of trade goods.

Just beyond the mouth of the Platte River, they met a man coming down the river. It proved to be John Colter who had been part of the Lewis and Clark Expedition. He had been away from civilization for three years, but now he joined Lisa's party as guide back to the upper Missouri country.

At the Arikara earthlodge villages, Lisa stopped when the Indians fired in front of his keelboat. With two swivel cannons pointed at the threatening Indians, Lisa went ashore, smoked the peace pipe, traded, then went up the river. Later, he found the Mandans and the Assiniboins showing a hostile attitude. He fired shot into the air, and the Indians smoked the peace pipe with him, then exchanged gifts.

Lisa established a trading post where the Big Horn and Yellowstone Rivers joined; he left young Colter in charge. He returned to St. Louis and there organized the Missouri Fur Company. Returning to the upper Missouri, he built Fort Lisa for trade with the Mandans and Hidatsa. (Lisa was located 8 miles above where Stanton, North Dakota, now is. The fort site is covered by the waters of Lake Sakakawea.)

In May, 1812, Lisa established another post of interest to North Dakotans. This was located on the Missouri just south of the present state boundary, and it was called Fort Manuel Lisa. Here Lisa brought the first cows, hogs, and chickens ever transported on the upper Missouri River.

By the time the United States was fighting the War of 1812 with England, Lisa had built a string of posts along the Missouri, from Nebraska and into Montana. And while British traders from Canadian posts tried to turn Indians against the Americans, Lisa kept their friendship.

He kept their friendship because he tried to be a helper. He carried vegetable seeds which he gave to the Indians to provide them with more food. His blacksmiths did whatever work they could for the Indians and charged them nothing. Lisa lent traps. At his posts he provided shelter for old men too weak to follow their people on hunts. And so Indians traded willingly with Manuel Lisa.

In 1815 Lisa brought 43 chiefs and head men to St. Louis to enter treaties of friendship. Before his death in 1820, he had traveled 26,000 miles up and down the Missouri.

In fur trade history, Manuel Lisa is considered the greatest of the Missouri River fur traders.

4 - Finding the 49th Parallel

In 1816 Congress passed a law requiring that only American citizens could trade with Indians within the territorial boundaries of the United States. The law did not apply to traders in the northern and eastern part of North Dakota because this was British territory, drained by the Souris and Red Rivers.

But in October, 1818, England signed a treaty with the United States whereby the Red River area south of the 49th parallel would become United States territory.

Where was the 49th parallel? In 1823 Major Stephen H. Long took charge of an expedition that would survey for the 49th parallel.

He started up the Minnesota River valley, escorted by soldiers. At Big Stone Lake the Wahpeton Sioux honored the white men with a dog feast, but where Abercrombie now is, another band of Sioux fired across their path.

Eager to get out of the Sioux hunting grounds, the expedition marched an average of 24 miles a day, going chiefly along the Minnesota side of the Red River. They arrived at Pembina on August 5 and found the village of log cabins and bark huts deserted. The next day most of the village people returned with their 115 Red River Carts screeching under 300-pound loads of buffalo meat and hides.

Who were these people? They were the **Metis**— part Indian and part French. French trappers and traders had married Indian women and their descendants were known as the Metis.

Before the Long expedition reached Pembina, the Hudson's Bay Company had suspected their trading post was in American territory. They had surveyed and found that indeed it was. So these British traders had moved north of the 49th parallel, leaving the trading post buildings. The Metis people had moved into the vacant buildings.

James C. Calhoun, the Long Expedition astronomer, soon determined the 49th parallel. Then he set up an oak post for a boundary marker. On the north side of the post he carved "G. B." for Great Britain, and on the south side of the post, "U. S."

This done, Major Long led his expedition home. But because a season of drouth had parched the prairies and dried up many streams, Long called Dakota "The Great American Desert."

5 - Getting Big White Home

The Arikaras failed to keep peace with the Mandans and went on the warpath against them. When a keelboat captained by Nathaniel Pryor in 1807 came up the Missouri to bring Chief Big White back to his Mandan people, the Arikaras learned that the Mandan chief was aboard and attacked. They killed three of the fur traders traveling with Pryor and wounded seven.

Pryor returned to St. Louis and declared that an escort of four hundred men would be needed to get Big White safely past the Arikaras. Big White, back in white man's society again, lived like a celebrity while U. S. Government officials tried to solve the problem of getting him home.

It was Manuel Lisa's Missouri Fur Company that finally succeeded in delivering Big White to his people. With over 150 men as escort, a brigade of nine keelboats and a canoe left St. Louis in the summer of 1809. This time the Arikaras made no attempt to capture Big White.

After they had deposited Chief Big White in his own earthlodge, the Missouri Fur Company collected $7000 from the Government for their accomplishment—a cost almost three times that of the Lewis and Clark Expedition.

After more than two years of being an honored guest among the palefaces, Chief Big White had too much to tell. His people simply could not believe all the wondrous things he told them. They decided he had been with the white man too long and had learned to speak with a "split tongue."

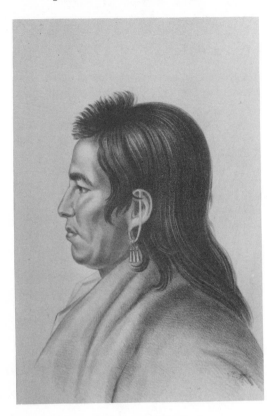

45—Chief Big White

6 - The Yellowstone Expeditions

After Lewis and Clark had planted the American flag on the Pacific coast, Americans wanted to establish a trade route to Asia by way of the Missouri River and the west- flowing Columbia River. They especially wanted military protection in the upper Missouri territory to keep out the trespassing British fur traders.

Ever since Robert Fulton in 1807 built a steamboat that successfully chugged up the Hudson River from New York to Albany and back, Americans dreamed as well of steamboats that could cross the Atlantic without the help of sails.

In 1819 the Yellowstone Expedition organized under the command of General Henry Atkinson. Five steamboats would carry eight hundred soldiers and a number of scientists up the Missouri.

But only one of the five steamboats, the **Western Engineer**, was designed for the shallow waters of Big Muddy. Not one of the steamboat pilots had ever sailed the treacherous river. And the Expedition was three months too late to take advantage of the June water rise.

Two of the steamboats never reached the Missouri. Two steamboats got no further than the mouth of the Kansas River. The **Western Engineer** hit a top speed of three miles per hour and reached Council Bluffs after having been grounded time and again on sandbars and often towed by men on shore.

Thus ended the First Yellowstone Expedition. It cost $250,000—a hundred times more than the Lewis and Clark Expedition.

Six years later, General Henry Atkinson took command of the Second Yellowstone Expedition. This time the

Expedition wanted only to make peace treaties with the Indians living along the Missouri River. No smoke-belching steamboats, but 80 sturdy keelboats—with man-powered paddlewheels—provided transportation for most of the 400 soldiers. Forty military men rode horseback along the river.

As they met with each tribe, the Expedition soldiers paraded. They fired the cannon. At night rockets exploded into the sky. Then they presented gifts to each chief. After such displays of power and good will, the Oglala Sioux, the Arikaras, and the Crows each agreed to peace.

Plagued by mosquitoes, the Expedition continued 120 miles up the Yellowstone River, but found no trace of Indians. They returned to St. Louis without trouble. There General Atkinson reported twelve treaties signed, no evidence of British intruders, and not one Expedition man or boat lost.

7 - King of the Upper Missouri

There came now a time of heavy fur trading which would nearly eradicate animals which during Indian times had lived in great numbers over the North Dakota prairies.

In 1822 James Kipp and a Mr. Tilton established a fur trade post on the east side of the Missouri opposite the Mandan villages. A year later some Arikaras chased Kipp out of his Fort Tilton. Kipp found refuge in the Mandan villages and traded there until 1827. Here he also married a daughter of the famous Chief Four Bears.

Kipp next moved to the White Earth River where he opened Kipp's Post and traded with the Assiniboins.

A German immigrant, John Jacob Astor, arrived in America with four flutes in his baggage. He bartered these flutes for trinkets and started trading for furs. He organized the American Fur Company. After establishing himself in business on the Columbia River in Oregon, he decided to do business on the upper Missouri River, too. So he sent Kenneth McKenzie in 1828 to build Fort Union three miles up the Missouri from the Yellowstone, just a few hundred yards east of the present Montana-North Dakota boundary.

Built on a wide prairie bench overlooking the river, Fort Union measured 220 feet square. Stone blockhouses 30 feet high, on opposite corners of the 20-foot high stockade, gave protection against Indian attack. The stockade enclosed barracks, storehouses, workshops, stables, a stone powder-house, and a large place for trading. Old Glory flew from a handsome staff in the center court. Brass cannon beside the flagstaff aimed at the gates.

For McKenzie there was built a handsome two-story log house. It boasted glass windows, a white-pillared porch and inside walls covered with red wallpaper and carpets on the floor.

Kenneth McKenzie soon came to be known as the King of the Upper Missouri. He dressed in handsome red or blue uniforms decorated with gold braid. His dining table boasted sterling silver and a damask cloth. He went to bed late and he got up late, but none of his employees could eat breakfast until the King of the Upper Missouri had been fed.

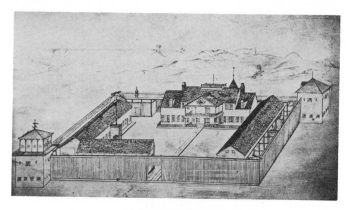

47—Drawing of Fort Union

48—Indians coming to Fort Union to trade   (Bodmer)

46—Kenneth McKenzie

He took as wife the daughter of an Assiniboin chief and dressed her and their children in fashionable clothes.

He held control over a wilderness territory larger than some European countries. He ruled more than a hundred men at Fort Union. Many of these men he sent out to trade and establish outposts both east and west of Fort Union.

When Lewis and Clark had lived with the Mandans, they learned that the earthlodge people wanted nothing to do with liquor. Captain Lewis wrote in his diary: "They say we are no friends or we would not give them what makes them fools."

But most fur traders in the upper Missouri country used the "firewater" to get Indians to trade their furs for less. Congress then passed a law that no liquor could be transported into Indian territory.

At Fort Union, the King of the Upper Missouri did not want to give up the advantage that liquor provided in trading with the Indians. He observed that the law did not allow the transportation of

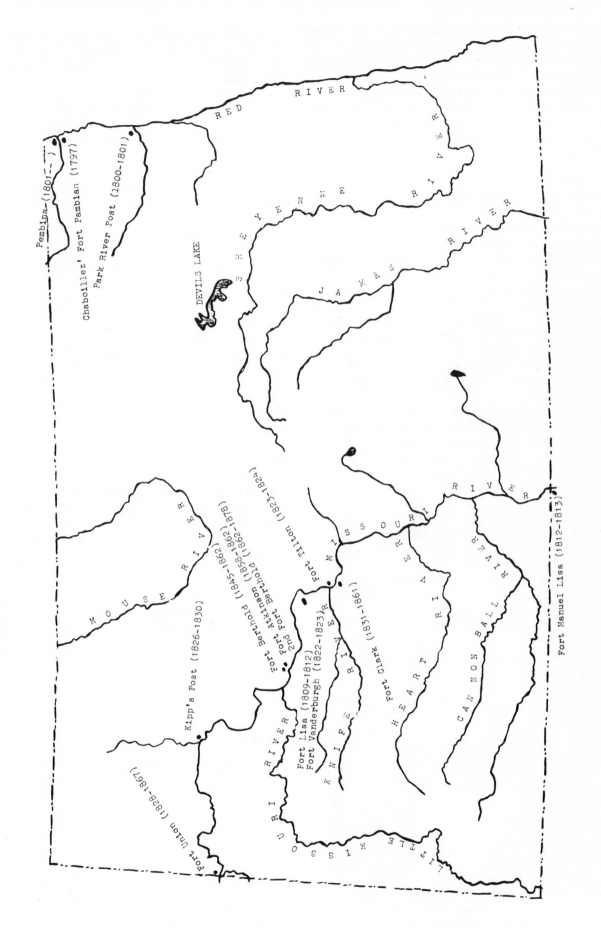

49—Fur trading posts in the North Dakota area (Author)

liquor; the law said nothing against manufacturing liquor! So he built a still at Fort Union, traded corn from the Mandan Indians, and produced a liquor that could make fools of any Indians who drank it.

Other competing fur traders smuggled liquor into the territory. This they diluted with Missouri river water and mixed in black chewing tobacco, red peppers, ginger, and black molasses. With such firewater at a Crow Indian camp, a trader was able to barter one keg of alcohol for fifty buffalo robes.

Learning what was happening at Fort Union, Congress passed a law prohibiting the making of firewater in Indian territory. McKenzie soon after left his Fort Union empire and returned to St. Louis. Another man took his place at Fort Union.

During McKenzie's rule at Fort Union, he shipped down the Missouri each year in 100-pound packs 25,000 muskrat pelts, between 40 and 50,000 buffalo robes, 20,000 to 30,000 deer hides, plus many other animal skins then in demand.

Working under McKenzie's supervision, James Kipp started other outposts for the American Fur Company. In the North Dakota area, he built Fort Clark. This station continued in the fur business for thirty years.

A good cat was a prized possession at these trading posts. While a cat might keep a dwelling free of mice, it could hardly control the rat population. At Fort Clark, one of the traders killed a total of 3,729 rats. The most he trapped in one month was 294 in October, 1836.

After the fur trader would come the homesteader who also trapped and hunted to earn money. For those who live in North Dakota today where there is a skycraper capitol, cities, plowed fields and pastures, it is difficult to believe that once this prairie land was home for thousands, even millions, of wild animals.

Islands, like sand bars, came and went. A new channel cut across rich bottom lands covered with willow and cottonwood trees and left the old channel filled with silt. This, in turn, grew over with willows and cottonwoods which would be uprooted when the playful Missouri romped that way again. Acres of rich bottom land disappeared into the river in a short season, sometimes in a matter of days. The site of Lewis and Clark's Fort Mandan long ago vanished into the river.

As the river ate into a bank, it undermined trees and tumbled them into the stream. Carried by the water current, these uprooted trees anchored in the bottom—sometimes above and sometimes below the surface. Only in clear weather could such dead trees be spied by a ripple. Riding up and down with the current, such "sawyer" trees caught in the river's bottom could rise up under a small boat and tip it over. Under a keelboat or steamer, a sawyer tree could rip through the bottom.

The Missouri River has two floods. The first comes with the melting of snow along its valley. The second flood is known as the June Rise and comes from the melting snows of the western mountains.

Prairie winds would fill the air with sand and dust from naked sand bars and shore. A strong wind could lash the river into such fury that small boats would tie up to a cottonwood tree for safety. Wind and rain made it about impossible to spy out uprooted trees under water.

Yet for almost a century this wily river served as a main highway for the white man coming into Dakota land and to the regions westward.

For the prairie Indian, the Missouri was his Grandmother River. If a summer drouth dried the creeks, Grandmother River could be depended upon for drinking water. The trees along her banks provided fuel and shelter in winter, and shade from summer heat. And the white man's boats that came traveling upon Grandmother River could bring friend or foe.

8 - Big Muddy

Those who look out over Lake Sakakawea today can little imagine what the Missouri River was like many years ago when fur traders and explorers traveled it. For the Garrison Dam tamed the Big Muddy.

Having no hard bed to hold it in place, the Missouri flowed through soft soil and looked like "bad coffee colored with condensed milk." The shoreline receded where the bulldozing current wore away the bank, while another shoreline—or a sand bar—built up where loosened soil came to rest.

The river channel shifted from one bluff to another, and developed many and unusual bends. At floodtide the waters poured across the neck of a narrow bend and cut a new channel across and created a new island.

9 - Fireboat upon the Water

Each year more steamers appeared on the Great Lakes and on the Mississippi. Though steamboats had failed for the First Yellowstone Expedition, American Fur Company men believed a steamer could be built that would serve better than the keelboat.

So they built a steamer they thought would be able to navigate the shallow Missouri. They named it **Yellowstone** for the river they wanted it to reach. A single-engine sidewheeler, the boat measured 130 feet long. Loaded to its capacity of 75 tons, it lay 5 1/2 feet into the water.

On its first voyage the summer of 1831, the **Yellowstone** got no further than the present location of Pierre, South Dakota. But the following year it steamed up the Missouri to Fort Union, unloaded its cargo and hustled back to St. Louis.

A year later the **Yellowstone** went up the Missouri again, this time accompanied by another steamer, the **Assiniboine**, and steamboat traffic on the Big Muddy began in earnest.

The arrival of steamers at river posts became festive times. When Fort Union sighted a boat coming, guns in the stone blockhouses thundered a welcome. The boat guns answered with a booming salute.

The steamboat brought news from the outside world, letters from home, merchandise and provisions for isolated men. Everyone at the fort crowded down to the docks. Deck hands and fort employees worked without stopping until goods were stored in the fort and the packs of fur put aboard the steamboat.

Soon after unloading, the boat started down the 1700 miles to St. Louis. The season of travel could end as the waters of the June Rise emptied down the stream.

The early steamers required a great amount of wood fuel. To supply this, boatmen went ashore to cut wood. But soon "woodhawks" stationed themselves along the river. These men cut down trees, sawed them into cordwood lengths, then stacked them at the river's edge. The woodhawks lived a lonely life and in danger of Indian braves wanting scalps. A woodhawk was safer if he took from a neighboring tribe a young woman to share his simple cabin. In the fall and winter, the woodhawk trapped and hunted so that when the steamer came in the spring, he had both wood and furs to sell.

For the Indian, the first appearance of a steamer on Grandmother River presented an awesome and frightening sight. Smoke belched from its stack, paddle wheels churned, the steam engine puffed and wheezed. Some called it the "big medicine canoe with eyes" for did it not see its own way into the deepest waters?

As a steamboat neared an earthlodge village, cannons aboard were fired in rapid succession so their noise echoed from river bluffs and the Mandans named it the "big thunder canoe."

A steamboat captain sometimes considered it amusing to let out a frightful discharge of steam from the escape pipe when he spotted Indians peering over a river bluff at the great mystery out in the river. At this, some Indians laid their faces to the ground; others ran in fearful haste. But as the number of steamers increased, Indians became accustomed to the big thunder canoes and joined the palefaces when the ship docked.

50—The Yellowstone on the Missouri (Bodmer)

51—Snags in the Missouri (Bodmer)

10 - Upper Missouri Guests

A young artist, George Catlin, boarded the Yellowstone because he wanted to paint and write about Indians. He stayed for a short time at Fort Clark and at Fort Union. Out on the prairies, he watched Indians both at work and at play—and he painted pictures of them. For eight years he visited many American tribes, taking notes for a book he later published. He painted hundreds of Indian portraits and scenes.

Maximilian, the German Prince of Wied, came up the Big Muddy on a steamer because he wanted to study plant and animal life along the upper Missouri. He brought with him a servant, and also an artist, Karl Bodmer. After a short stay at Fort Union, Prince Maximilian went down river to Fort Clark. Here he and Bodmer and the servant lived in a log cabin during the winter of 1833-1834.

Because of his professional training as a naturalist, Maximilian wrote dependable accounts of the natural history of the region. Bodmer's skillful

52—Drawing showing George Catlin painting an Indian portrait

53—Mandan men playing their favorite game of "Tchung-kee" (Catlin)

drawings of Indians and animal life are treasured today even as they excited Americans and Europeans of his day.

The famous naturalist, John James Audubon, stayed at Fort Union in 1843. Out on the prairies he found eleven species of birds unknown to scientists.

The Jesuit priest, Father Pierre Jean de Smet, traveled the upper Missouri on early steamers, stopping at Indian villages, trading posts, and military forts, and ministering to whites and Indians. He worked as a peacemaker among the Indians.

An English sportsman, John Palliser, came to Fort Union in 1848 and hunted in the area. He collected specimens of mountain sheep in the Badlands and shot five grizzly bears in the Killdeer Mountains.

The Irish adventurer, Sir George Gore, arrived at Fort Union in 1856 with his 40 servants and guides, 112 horses, 6 wagons, several yoke of oxen, 40 dogs and 21 carts. He had spent nearly three years in the

Western wilderness. When Fort Union officials overcharged him for flatboats, he burned his wagons and goods in front of the fort, and gave away his horses to Indians and some roaming whites. Then he sailed down river to Fort Berthold. Here he remained until spring when he and his servants boarded a steamer for St. Louis.

11 - Plague upon the Prairies

In June, 1837, the **St. Peter** docked at Fort Clark, its watchman dying of smallpox. To keep the disease from the Indians, the captain ordered that no Indian should come aboard.

But this order made one Mandan chief suspicious. He sneaked aboard and stole a blanket from the bed of the dying man. When this theft was reported, the chief was offered a new blanket in exchange—but the infected blanket could not be found.

The **St. Peter** steamed on to Fort Union, leaving behind the germs of a disease against which Indians had no defense. The disease spread easily among the earthlodge people because they lived close together. Within a short time, the Mandan tribe of 1600 Indians was reduced to only fifty. Carried to the neighboring Hidatsa and Arikara earthlodges, these too were reduced to just a fraction of their population.

Aboard the **St. Peter**, other men fell ill with smallpox. Assiniboin Indians had encamped near Fort Union to be ready for trading. When they began approaching the fort, traders and interpreters rode out to meet them with trade goods so they could trade away from the fort where smallpox had brought death. The traders warned the Assiniboins not to come close to the fort, but they ignored the warning, insisting on doing business as usual at the fort. So they camped just outside the fort.

Before the week had passed, cartloads of dead were dumped into the river. That summer brought death to 4000 Assiniboins. In darkness and daylight the pestilence of smallpox stalked from tepee to tepee, from earthlodge to earthlodge. From band to band, tribe to tribe, the smallpox horror followed those who tried to run from it. When the disease had spent itself a year later, about 15,000 upper Missouri Indians had died from it. (There had been earlier smallpox epidemics among the Indians in 1781 and 1801, but far fewer had died then.)

Scattered widely over the prairies, the Sioux did not suffer as much from the pestilence. While the Assiniboins did not blame the white men, the Sioux and the Mandan hearts "were bad" toward the white men they held responsible.

But the smallpox scourge of 1837-1838 broke the strength of most tribes in the upper Missouri. Death broke up families and clans. Weakened, the Sioux agreed to give up to the United States all the land they claimed east of the Mississippi River. In return the U. S. Government promised to pay an annual indemnity of $40,000 for the next twenty years.

Money the Indian could not understand or use. He could not go to Eastern markets to buy what he needed. He had no way of transporting goods from the East. So the Indian agent entered into the Indian's life, and the Indian would have to accept whatever the agent doled out to him.

The Mandans and Hidatsa, now of small numbers, became more than friendly neighbors. They decided to live together in one village. Thus in 1844 they built their Like-a-Fishhook village on a fish-hook-shaped point of land jutting into Grandmother River from the east, many miles up from Fort Clark and their desolated villages. In 1862 the Arikaras also built their lodges in the northern part of Like-a- Fishhook village.

Though the three farmer tribes lived in the same community, they kept their separate ways. Each spoke a different language. Each tribe kept its particular customs and traditions. They did not intermarry. Each tribe felt superior to the other tribes. Arikara boys would tease and fight Mandan boys, or rob the Hidatsa girls of corn cobs while the girls guarded their cornfields. But let the Sioux threaten their village, and the three tribes joined as one in defense.

55—Four Bears, the noted Mandan chief   (Bodmer)

56—Hidatsa warrior   (Bodmer)

54—Assiniboin warrior   (Bodmer)

V - Red River Valley Beginnings

1 - The Selkirkers

Late in the fall of 1812, the first homeseekers came to North Dakota. Scottish Highlanders, they had tramped 70 miles from Fort Douglas (where Winnipeg, Canada, now is).

They came seeking buffalo meat and shelter for the winter. They knocked at the door of Pembina House, the fur post of the North West Company. The trader listened as they told him how they had lost their homes in the Old Country and had come to find new ones in the New Land.

For centuries their ancestors had lived as tenant farmers on the great estates of British nobility. Then the spinning jenny and the power loom brought wool into great demand. The nobles who owned the land could make more money by turning fields into pasture for sheep—and sheep needed only a few shepherds to care for them.

So the landowners evicted 450,000 tenants from their estates. The houses of 15,000 peasants had been put to the torch in the Highlanders' home parish of Kildonan.

But another Scottish nobleman, Lord Douglas, the Earl of Selkirk, had gained control of a large part of the Hudson's Bay Company territory—and here he wanted to settle Highlander peasants who had no place to go. The first shipload of such peasants (known as Selkirkers) in 1811 found no welcome among the fur traders at York Factory on Hudson Bay. No provisions or shelter awaited them.

They built rude shelters for their first winter. Only 22 of the 70 colonists lived until spring. Friendly Indians encouraged the survivors to go farther south into the Red River Valley. For 55 days that spring they struggled down to the forks of the Red and Assiniboine Rivers. There they built their Fort Douglas.

Having no provisions for their second winter, they set out for Pembina where, the Indians said, there would be buffalo. When they reached Pembina, the friendly trader helped them as best he could. Near Pembina the Selkirkers built a cluster of thatch-roofed log huts and surrounded them with a palisade and called it Fort Daer. They had not completed their building when sixty more settlers - men, women, and children - joined them.

Being British subjects, they returned in the spring to their Fort Douglas in Canada and there tried to farm. More shiploads of Selkirkers would come in the next years. They came seeking neither gold nor furs, only a piece of land on which to build homes and grow crops.

But those who did business with furs wanted no farmers because they would drive fur-bearing animals away. When actual warfare broke out between the men of competing fur companies, some innocent Selkirkers were killed. Some Selkirkers, discouraged, left Fort Douglas and migrated to St. Paul, Minnesota, where they settled. Several Selkirkers who had wintered at Pembina, set out on snowshoes for Prairie du Chien. There they loaded small boats with wheat, oats, and barley, and a few chickens. Up the Mississippi, Minnesota, and Red Rivers they went with the seed that would finally establish them as farmers in the Red River Valley in Canada.

2 - Pembina Hunters

For about seventy-five years, the descendants of French men and Indian wives gathered twice a year at Pembina. Entire families of these **Metis** people came down from Canada to go on buffalo hunts in what is now North Dakota. They crossed the international boundary line as though it did not exist.

They came on foot, on horseback, or in their squealing Red River Carts, their dogs frisking along. Once all the Metis families had reached Pembina, they made their first camp on the prairies west of the trading post.

The largest of these yearly Pembina Hunts took place the summer of 1840. The expedition consisted of 620 hunters, 650 women, and 360 children. Each hunter had a horse for hunting and at least one cart drawn by an ox or another horse.

At the first encampment each year, the hunters chose ten captains. Each captain had ten soldiers under his command. These soldiers served as policemen to keep order in camp and on the march.

Each guide took his turn in leading the expedition for a day. When the guide hoisted his flag in the morning, this signaled the camp to get ready to move.

Regulations usually ordered that no person could hunt by himself. Nor could any small party set off by itself. No hunter could start for a buffalo herd until the captain gave orders to go.

Once the expedition got under way, the screeching of the ungreased cart wheels could be heard several miles. A wide line of carts started the procession. Space between cart lines allowed the dust to settle. Thus the entire procession of spaced cart lines could stretch out as much as five or six miles.

When the guide lowered his flag in the evening, the captain and soldiers took charge, directing carts into a huge circle. Within one end of the circle, the women set up tents in a row. In hostile Indian country, the oxen and horses were corralled in the opposite part of the enclosed camp grounds. Otherwise, they grazed outside under the watch of soldiers.

In the evening, the leading men held council outside the ring of carts. Within the circle, women and men, dressed in festive garments, danced.

Not until they had traveled for 19 days did the Pembina Hunters of 1840 come upon their first herd of buffaloes. Each hunter mounted his horse and waited for the captain's signal. His bullet pouch and powder horn and knife hung ready at his side. He kept three or four bullets in his mouth. And he was able to reload his gun while riding his galloping horse among wild buffaloes.

After the captain had surveyed the buffalo herd through his spyglass, he yelled, "Ho! Ho!" and the hunters all started off at a slow trot, not wanting to excite the buffalo herd. When the hunters reached about five hundred yards from them, the buffalo bulls began to paw the ground, curve their tails, and then run. Now the hunters took after them at full speed.

As the hundreds of buffaloes and horses pounded away, the earth seemed to shudder under the thundering hooves. Dust rose into the air in darkening, thickening clouds.

Ten feet or so from his prey, a hunter shot so as to strike the buffalo's heart. The instant the shot was fired, his horse would leap aside to keep from stumbling upon the falling buffalo.

In the clouds of dust, the hunters rode in every direction, criss-crossing one another's paths in pursuit of one particular animal. Shots could whiz in front of a hunter, at his side, or behind him. If a horse stumbled, its rider could fall to the ground. An enraged bull could gore a fallen hunter to death.

Because of many rocks and badger holes on the 1840 hunt, 23 hunters were thrown to the ground. Bulls gored one horse to death, crippled two others. But after a total of 1,315 buffalo killed, only three hunters were injured, none killed.

57—Metis family traveling in their Red River Cart (Illustration in Harper's Monthly Magazine, June, 1879)

At the end of the chase, each hunter jumped from his horse, looped bridle reins over his shoulders, and set to work skinning the last buffalo he had shot. Then he retraced his way among the carcasses, identifying his own.

Families followed with the carts onto which they loaded meat and skins claimed by their own hunter. At camp the women cut the meat into strips and hung these to dry on pole racks. The meat dried for a day or more in the sun and wind. The dried meat strips were then dropped into large kettles of boiling tallow. The mixture of tallow and meat strips was poured hot into buffalo hide sacks and sewn shut. Once this pemmican had hardened, it could be stored for several years.

Their hunting done in North Dakota, the Metis went merrily back to their homes in Canada.

3 - Nicollet

For nearly half a century the little village of Pembina was the only settlement in the entire northeastern part of North Dakota. After Major Long's survey had placed the oak post boundary marker just north of the village, the Selkirkers moved north to Fort Douglas because they were British subjects. Then the Metis moved into the cabins built by the Selkirkers and lived there.

Aside from tales brought back by a few adventurers and traders, Americans knew little about the Red River Valley. So the U. S. War Department hired a French scientist, Jean N. Nicollet, to explore and gather information about the unknown territory between the Missouri River and the Mississippi River headwaters. A young Army engineer, Lt. John C. Fremont, who later gained fame as the Pathfinder of the Southwest, went along to help Nicollet.

Nicollet and Fremont traveled up from St. Louis on the American Fur Company's river steamer, **Antelope**. At Fort Pierre (in what is now South Dakota), the 19 members of the expedition started out on July 3, 1839, with ten wagons and thirty horses.

They entered the North Dakota area in the Oakes vicinity. Going northward along the James River, they crossed over to the Sheyenne River and followed northward to a placid lake which Fremont named Lake Jessie in honor of the girl he was to marry.

In the Sheyenne River country, an immense herd of buffalo slowed the expedition's travel for three days. While they pushed through the buffalo, they came upon an encampment of 2,000 Sioux. The expedition reached Devils Lake on July 29. The party then turned south along the upper branches of the Goose and Maple Rivers, crossed the Sheyenne where Lisbon now is, and left the North Dakota territory on August 16.

When Major Long's expedition had gone to Pembina in 1823 to survey for the 49th parallel, the country had been hot and dry. So Major Long had reported that the Red River Valley was not a place in which people should settle. But when Nicollet and Fremont explored, they found the prairie green and lush and declared the territory an excellent place for settlement.

58—Joe Rolette

4 - Jolly Joe Rolette

Born at Prairie du Chien to a fur trader, Joe Rolette was sent to New York to get an education. New Yorkers stared when Joe came there and walked down the streets in his buckskin suit, with his rifle over his shoulder. Joe went to school, but when he had grown up, he returned to the frontier country where he felt most at home.

In 1841 he went to Pembina to become a trader for the American Fur Company. Here he married a gentle Metis girl. His fur trade station became the center of Pembina life. The Chippewa Indians who came there to trade named Joe "Prairie Chicken's Son." Fun-loving and kind, Joe took part in Chippewa dances and jigged with his Metis friends. When winter cold made life rather dull, he hitched his half-wild dogs to a sled. Dressed in furs, he drove off to Saint Paul.

Because of Joe's friendliness to them, many of the Metis people left Canada and lived at Pembina. To get his furs to market, Joe decided to use the squealing carts his Metis friends had made. Constructed entirely of wood, the carts had two wheels measuring five feet in diameter. Each high-bodied cart could carry up to half a ton. One driver would hitch several carts in tandem and travel up to twenty miles a day.

In 1843 he set out for Saint Paul with several carts loaded with furs. Thus began the Red River Cartways on which Red River Valley commerce would depend for freight transportation until river steamers and railways took over.

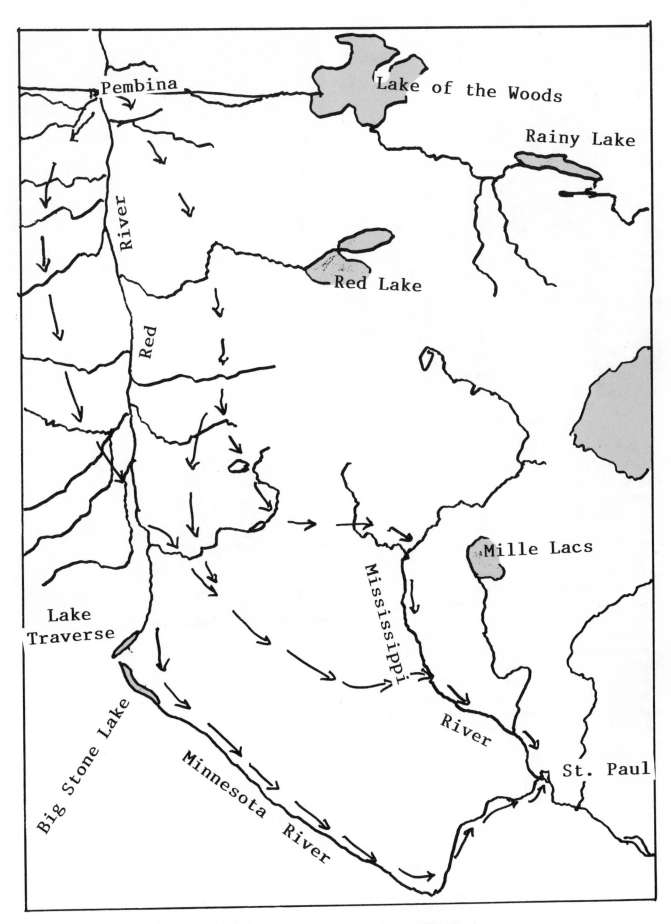

59—Red River Cartways trails from Pembina to Saint Paul
(Author)

60—Norman W. Kittson

61—Kittson's fur-trade cabin. The oldest building in North Dakota, it is located in Walhalla State Park. (Raymond Melin photo)

5 - *The Red River Cartways*

In 1844 Norman W. Kittson came to Pembina to manage the fur trade business. He liked Joe Rolette's use of Red River carts for transporting furs and trade goods.

Ten years after Joe took the first carts to Saint Paul, more than a hundred carts made the trip each year. This number increased so that by 1868 more than 2500 carts carried freight the 500 miles between Pembina and Saint Paul.

Kittson hired the Metis to handle the carts. Accustomed to driving their carts on buffalo hunts, these hardy people took naturally to the cartways, willing to endure the hardships of the long journey. Entire families traveled along.

In wet weather, the cart wheels sank into heavy mud and marshlands. For this reason some drivers followed a route along higher ground west of the Red River. A second route went along the prairie on the east side of the Red. A third way dodged through the Minnesota woods to the Mississippi River and then to Saint Paul.

Swarms of mosquitoes often tortured horses, oxen, dogs, and people. In order to escape the insects, the drivers wrapped themselves in blankets no matter how hot the day might be. Through floods and blistering heat, the Metis drove their trains 15 to 20 miles a day. When they camped at night, they sang French songs and danced around their campfires. When at length they reached Saint Paul, the Red River Cart drivers and their families delighted in the sights of the growing city, and townsfolk and travelers delighted in them.

Story of the Peace Garden State, page 38

62—Train of Red River Carts hitched together

6 - "St. Joe"

Thirty miles west of Pembina, Kittson established another trading post called St. Joseph. To this little settlement in 1848 came a young Presbyterian minister, Alonzo Barnard. He brought with him the first printing press and the first melodeon ever brought to North Dakota.

Other missionaries also arrived at St. Joseph. Two were killed by the Sioux and one died of pneumonia. Known today as the "Martyrs of St. Joe," they are buried in a cemetery near Walhalla.

When furs became scarce and buffaloes no longer came near, the little settlement of St. Joseph ceased to be. In 1877, a new town was established in the same place and took the name of Walhalla.

In Pembina, Father George Belcourt reopened the Catholic mission and later established another mission at St. Joseph. To St. Joseph he brought the first church bell to ring in North Dakota. This bell continues in use at St. Boniface Catholic Church at Walhalla.

At Pembina, Belcourt also directed the building of the first flour mill in North Dakota. Powered by the Pembina River, this mill served the farmers there for many years.

7 - The Woods Expedition

British fur traders unlawfully sneaked across the border to hunt and to trade with Indians. They also supplied Indians with liquor which was against American law. At Fort Garry in Canada, British soldiers stood ready to protect the Selkirkers, but there was no military protection for the nearly thousand Metis people in the Pembina area.

For generations, the plains Indian people had depended on Uncle Buffalo for food, clothing, and shelter. They now foresaw how the whites were slaughtering the buffalo and thus bringing an end to the Indian way of life. At Pembina, Father Belcourt could understand that the Sioux might well rise up to destroy the white people who were destroying their Uncle Buffalo.

So Belcourt wrote to the U. S. Commissioner of Indian Affairs at Washington, D. C., and asked that military protection be brought to the Red River Valley. Jonathan E. Fletcher, an Indian agent on the upper Missouri, joined in that appeal.

Accordingly, Major Samuel Woods headed an expedition into the Red River Valley in 1849. He was to find a suitable place for a military fort, and get facts about the British illegal trespassing.

The Expedition left Fort Snelling on June 6. Clouds of mosquitoes tortured the men as they came into the Red River Valley. Mosquitoes swirled about them when they set up a square post where Fort Abercrombie would be built. They marked the post "163 miles to Sauk Rapids, July 14, 1849."

They marched northward, passing by a vast herd of buffalo grazing near the Goose River. At Pembina they learned that the Selkirkers in the lower Red River Valley in Canada harvested 30 to 40 bushels of wheat to the acre, 40 to 50 bushels of barley and oats, and 200 to 300 bushels of potatoes. So the Expedition men recognized that the Red River Valley within the United States would make fertile farming land.

After much rain, the Red River now flooded 20 feet above its banks. The Expedition wagons mired down on the open prairies as they returned to Fort Snelling.

Nothing happened as a result of the Woods Expedition. For the next quarter of a century, Pembina and St. Joseph continued as the only pockets of American settlement in that part of the United States.

But the same year that the Woods Expedition came to Pembina, Norman W. Kittson was appointed the first postmaster. Two years later, Charles T. Cavileer came to serve as customs inspector at the border.

When Minnesota Territory was organized in 1849, a large part of it was called Pembina County. Pembina County then included all of North Dakota east of the Missouri and White Earth Rivers, as well as a part of northeastern South Dakota. The eastern boundary of Pembina County was a line going straight south from Lake of the Woods.

Kittson was appointed to serve as Pembina County Senator in this first Minnesota Territory legislature, and Jolly Joe Rolette as representative. To attend the sessions of the legislature in Saint Paul, the two men traveled by dog sled. While Kittson's dogs and sleds were plain and sturdy, Jolly Joe decorated his dogs with ribbons and tinkling bells.

8 - Stevens Railway Survey

With the discovery of gold in California, thousands of people headed that direction to "get rich quick." The first week of February, 1849, fifty ships sailed from eastern American ports and around the southern tip of South America and up the Pacific to San Francisco. Within three weeks of the spring of that year some 18,000 persons started overland for California, following the Oregon Trail much of the way.

While all Americans agreed that they needed a railway to cross the continent, they could not agree upon the route such a railway should take. People in the northern states were against slavery while people in the southern states used slave labor. A railway on a southern route could add more slave states and a railway on a northern route could add more states where slavery would be outlawed.

To help a railway company build this tremendously expensive railroad, Congress would give the railway company large grants of land along the route. To find which route would cost the least to build, it was decided to survey four possible routes.

Secretary of War Jefferson Davis assigned General Isaac Ingalls Stevens—who had been appointed governor of Washington Territory—to survey the northernmost route. Besides learning the best railway route, Stevens was also to make peace with unfriendly Indian tribes along the way,

63—Survey camp in Sheyenne River Valley (John M. Stanley engraving)

Stevens left Saint Anthony, Minnesota, May 20, 1853, with Pierre Bottineau as guide. The Expedition crossed the Red River into North Dakota territory in the Wahpeton vicinity. Shortly after crossing the Red River, Stevens met Kittson, Rolette, Cavileer, and a priest bound for Saint Paul, their Red River Carts loaded with furs and pemmican. From them Stevens bought several carts with their loads of buffalo meat.

The surveying expedition continued on a way which many years later would be followed by the builders of the Great Northern Railway. As they journeyed, the men hunted rabbits, prairie chickens and ducks to add to their regular rations. They found a herd of approximately 200,000 buffaloes crowding about Lake Jessie.

Westward by Dog Den Butte, they passed the south loop of the Souris River. In the Lostwood area they came upon a camp of 150 lodges of Assiniboins. The tribe asked for a treaty that would protect them from the Sioux.

The Stevens Expedition reached Fort Union on August 1. There they joined a part of the Expedition which had explored up the Missouri River by boat. They then continued westward to meet a survey expedition that had started eastward from Puget Sound.

While no railway resulted for many years, the Stevens men reported so enthusiastically about the fertile lands they had traveled through in Dakota that landseekers now began turning eyes toward the Red River Valley.

9 - Fort Abercrombie

In 1857, Colonel John J. Abercrombie built the first military fort in North Dakota at the place where Woods had left the marking post in 1849. Except for the brick and mortar powder magazine, the buildings were made of wood. All its supplies had to be brought from Saint Paul, 245 miles away over rough trails. Abercrombie and his men stayed at the fort during the winter, then abandoned it in the spring.

A year later, Joe Rolette and Norman Kittson lost their jobs as legislators when Minnesota became a state. The land east of the Missouri River to the Red River was then left out of any organized territory, and so became a sort of No Man's Land. Until soldiers returned to Fort Abercrombie in 1860, this territory had no direct government.

Beginning in 1859, a stagecoach company carried mail and passengers between St. Paul and Fort Abercrombie. The stagecoach then drove up the Red River Valley to Pembina, stopping at settlements along the way.

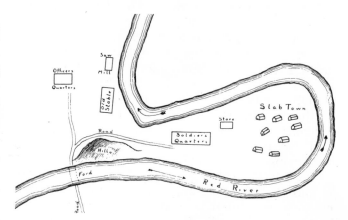

64—Drawing of Fort Abercrombie, 1858

10 - Thunder Canoes on the Red

Red River Carts transported goods from as far away as Fort Garry (where Winnipeg now is). Saint Paul business men watched these slow, lumbering carts come and go and wondered why a steamboat on the Red River could not do a better job. So the Saint Paul Chamber of Commerce offered $1000 to the first man who could get a steamboat operating on the Red River.

Anson Northrop, a Mississippi River boat owner, sailed his **North Star** up the Mississippi and then west as far as he could go on the Crow Wing River. He took the boat apart, and by late February he loaded the boat's mechanisms onto sleds drawn by 13 yoke of oxen and 17 teams of horses. Without a guide, Northrop set out with 31 men for the Red River about 150 miles due west.

By the first of April, 1859, Northrop had reached the Red River opposite the mouth of the Sheyenne. The men set to work cutting timbers from which they built the boat they re- named the **Anson Northrop**. Launched on the high waters of the spring thaw, this boat first made a trial run to Fort Abercrombie. then on June 5 started down the crooked river to Fort Garry.

Steam hissed from the leaking old locomotive boiler. Smoke and sparks belched from the funnel. The sternwheel threshed as the boat hurried along with its cargo of one hundred kegs of gunpowder. Along its way, it frightened Indians, sent buffaloes running with upturned tails, and bears scurrying for cover. But on June 9, the little steamboat reached Fort Garry.

Three days later, with 20 passengers aboard bound for the United States, the **Anson Northrop** returned up the Red to Fort Abercrombie. There Captain Northrop anchored his boat and hurried across country to Saint Paul to claim his prize of $1000. The Saint Paul Chamber of Commerce men were so happy about Northrop's boat, they doubled the prize money. Soon after, Northrop sold the first steamboat on the Red for $8000.

The buyers, J. C. Burbank and Company, sent a captain and crew to Fort Abercrombie. Shallow water and boulders in the Goose Rapids hindered the **Anson Northrop**'s second trip down the Red. When it reached Indian River, a short distance from Fort Garry, it had to be tied up for the winter.

Because it had been built of green timbers, it leaked badly the following spring. Repaired, it was christened the **Pioneer** and it did a fair amount of business that season.

Meanwhile, another man had also tried to win that $1000 prize for the first steamboat on the Red. Captain John B. Davis had started up the Minnesota River with his **Freighter**, thinking he could take the boat by high water through Big Stone Lake, Lake Traverse, and down the Bois des Sioux into the Red River. But the boat grounded a few miles above Big Stone Lake, and Davis left her in charge of a Welsh crewman.

A few years later, without even having a look at the boat, J. C. Burbank and Company bought the **Freighter**. When their crew arrived to take the boat apart and haul it overland to the Red River, they found the faithful Welshman still on guard. By this time, however, he had worn out his clothes and had made new ones from coffee sacking and the ship's curtains.

Rebuilt and renamed the **International**, this boat, too, did business on the Red. Meanwhile, the Chippewa Indians protested that these thunder canoes drove their game away and killed the fish in the river.

65—The Anson Northrop on the Red River

66—Aerial view of Red River showing one of the hundreds of curves making navigation difficult (Sheldon Green photo)

VI - Dakota Territory

1 - The Beginnings

On March 2, 1861, President James Buchanan signed a bill which created three territories: Dakota, Colorado, and Nevada. The name of Dakota was selected because it was the name by which the Sioux Indians called themselves, and they lived and hunted over most of the Territory.

As organized in 1861, Dakota Territory consisted of 360,000 square miles including the present states of North Dakota, South Dakota, Montana, and the northern half of Wyoming. During Dakota Territory's 28 years, its size and shape would change several times as new territories and states were formed from it.

Congress would control Dakota Territory. The President appointed Government officials. People living in the Territory had little voice in government.

Four small settlements (Bon Homme, Yankton, Vermillion, and Sioux Falls) clustered in the southeast corner of Dakota Territory on land obtained from the Sioux Indians in 1858. In the northeast corner was Pembina.

Abraham Lincoln became President on March 4, 1861. He selected the first Dakota Territory officers. Dr. William Jayne, from Springfield, Illinois, was made governor. John Hutchinson of Minnesota became secretary; Philemon Bliss of Ohio, chief justice; L. P. Williston of Pennsylvania and J. L. Williams of Tennessee, associate justices; W. F. Gleason of Maryland, attorney general; G. D. Hill of

68—Dr. William Jayne, first Dakota Territory governor

Michigan, surveyor general; Dr. W. A. Burleigh of Pennsylvania, agent for the Yankton Dakota Indians; and H. A. Hoffman of New York, agent for the Ponca Indians.

None of these men had ever seen Dakota. They did not know where the new capital would be, so they headed for Sioux City, Iowa. Here they learned that Governor Jayne had selected Yankton as the capital.

When they reached the capital city, these Territorial officials found Yankton a settlement of sod and log huts sheltering about 300 people. Most of these were unmarried young men who carried guns and knives on their persons.

67—Contemporary drawing of Yankton, Dakota Territory, 1861 (Moses K. Armstrong, Early Empire Builders of the Great West)

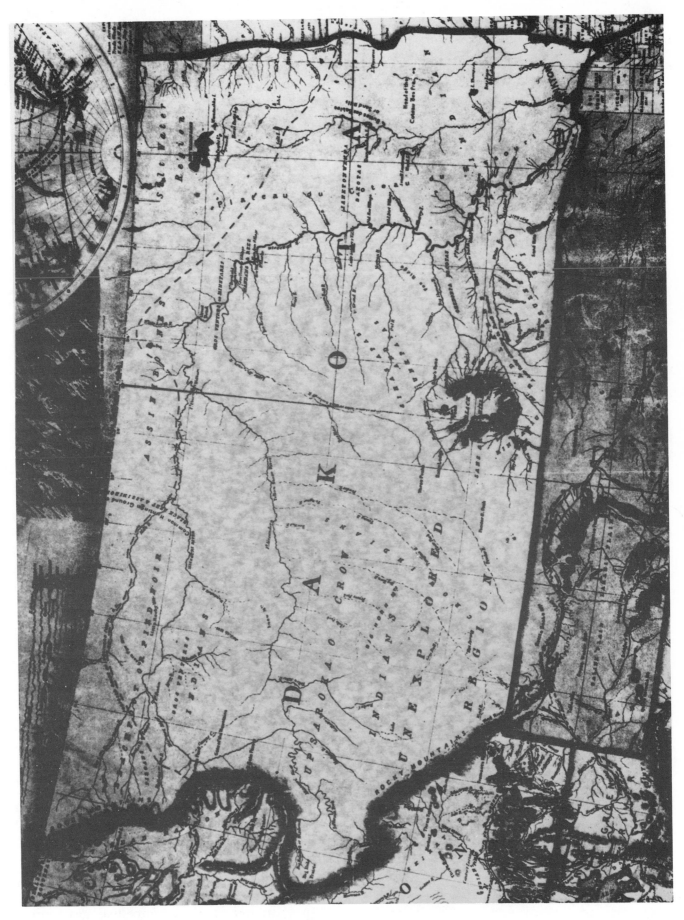

69—Dakota Territory as first organized in 1861

The officials found living quarters in the Ash Hotel. Hotel floors were of hard-packed earth. Blankets or hides divided the sleeping quarters into compartments where two or three men shared each bed. For the first six months, Governor Jayne shared a bed with Attorney General Gleason. A log cabin served as the governor's executive office.

Governor Jayne immediately ordered that a census be taken. The results showed a total population of 2,402. Living in what is now North Dakota were 514 mixedbloods and 76 whites, mostly in the Pembina area. The southeast corner of Dakota Territory had the largest population—1,186 of which only 46 were mixedbloods.

2 - Paleface Council

Only full-blooded white men were allowed to vote in the first election scheduled for September 16, 1861. The early political campaigns in Dakota Territory included mass meetings, torch light parades, Indian war dances, and even some shooting matches and a dog feast. In one situation, some one shot the candidate's hat off—but he went right on speaking.

Up at Pembina, Joe Rolette took a candidate for a ride in a Red River Cart to travel among the settlers there. At night after the electioneering, people danced and feasted on pemmican, maple sugar, rabbits and rum.

As soon as the election had taken place and members had been elected to the first Dakota Assembly, the Territorial officials all left Dakota Territory and went back to their homes in the East.

They returned when the first Dakota Territory legislature met on March 17, 1862. The representatives met in a clapboarded dwelling, and the senators in a small church. Parliamentary procedure allowed legislators to fire a pistol in order to get the speaker's attention. After some lively lawmaking, it was decided that Yankton would keep the capital, a university would be established at Vermillion, and a penitentiary at Bon Homme—all in the southeast corner of Dakota Territory.

70—Pistol-brandishing oratory during the first Dakota Assembly (Armstrong)

Most of these legislators were under thirty years of age. One of the most unusual of these men was Enos Stutsman, a man born with abnormally short legs. With the help of crutches, he could toss himself into a buggy or upon a horse's back. After serving in the legislature and as the governor's secretary, he took the job of U. S. Customs Inspector at Pembina—and there the people promptly elected him to serve as their representative in the legislature.

Dakota Territory had existed scarcely one month when Confederates fired on Fort Sumter, and the Civil War began.

71—Enos Stutsman

3 - The Homestead Act

The same year that Dakota Territory was created and the Civil War began, Congress passed a law which would bring thousands of settlers into Dakota Territory.

The Homestead Act of 1861 permitted any citizen over 21 (or an immigrant who intended to become a citizen) to get ownership of 160 acres of public land by legally taking possession of it, living on that 160 acres for five years, and making certain improvements on it.

(Joe Rolette was the first man to file on a homestead in what is now North Dakota. He did this on June 15, 1868, at the Vermillion land office.)

The Yankton band of Sioux had given up 4 million acres of land to the U. S. Government in exchange for annual food provisions and money payments. This area lay between the Big Sioux and

Missouri Rivers. Settlers began coming in great numbers into this area in the summer of 1862. Where Uncle Buffalo had been lord of the prairies for centuries, white men plowed fields and harvested bountiful crops. Settlers brought cattle and horses, sheep, hogs, roosters and hens and built barns, pastures, and corrals. Sod huts and log cabins made permanent homes where traveling tepees had camped.

4 - Yellow Dust down Grandmother River

In the first years of Dakota Territory, the discovery of gold in Montana and Idaho country lured white men into trespassing ever more into Indian lands. The safest way to these gold fields was by steamer up the Missouri.

The steamboat could best transport the heavy machinery needed for mining. The **Chippewa** and the **Key West** had reached Fort Benton in Montana in 1860, thus proving that steamers made for mountain rivers could carry freight to within 100 or 200 miles of the mines.

While Dakota Assembly men debated at Yankton, prospectors found gold dust and nuggets along Grasshopper Creek in southwestern Montana, the next year at Alder Gulch, and in the fall of 1864 a rich strike at Last Chance. In three years Alder Gulch became Virginia City with a population of 10,000 and the city of Helena grew out of the Last Chance camp. In 1865 more than $18,000,000 worth of gold was taken out of Montana mines.

By 1867 seventy ships traveled the Missouri, carrying tremendous amounts of annuities for Indians and provisions for military forts, thousands of tons of trade merchandise, many quartz mills, and hundreds of passengers.

On these river steamers, a boat master earned $200 a month, a clerk $150, an engineer $125. But a Missouri pilot could ask for $1000 a month and get it. A steamer's profits depended on the pilot's ability to "read water," thus to get the boat past snags, through the narrow and shifting channels of Big Muddy. Profits for boat owners could be enormous.

In 1866, for example, the **St. John** cleared a profit of $17,000 in one season, the **W. J. Lewis**, $40,000 and the **Peter Bolen** $65,000. The **Luella**, last boat to come down the river before freeze-up that year, carried 230 miners and the greatest single cargo of gold brought down the river—$1,250,000.

During the gold rush years, about 1200 miners each autumn left Montana as late as possible by coming down the river in mackinaw boats. Large fleets of these flat-bottomed boats traveled together for protection against Indians.

The Indians angrily watched this river traffic trespassing through their hunting grounds. They also learned that provisions intended for Indians somehow got into the hands of white traders. The sky-high prices miners paid for provisions caused many tons of supplies intended for the Indians to travel instead to a mining camp.

And so each summer Sioux Indians prowled along Grandmother River to collect the scalps of goldseekers. Bullets scarred steamers, but only a few men aboard were killed. Miners sailing downstream in the open mackinaw boats made easier targets, and sometimes victorius warriors dumped captured gold dust into the river.

5 - Misunderstanding

The settlers who moved into Dakota Territory (particularly the European immigrants) little understood the Indian's thinking and way of life. Most white men looked upon the Indian as a savage who needed to be made civilized.

The Dakota settler marked the boundaries of his 160-acre homestead with stones or stakes. He built fences to make pastures for his cattle and horses. The white settler said, "This is my land. You cannot hunt on my land."

This the Indian found hard to understand. How could land be owned—like a lariat or robe? Land was ground. It had sky above it. How could any man claim to own something which had existed before he was born and would be there after he died? The Indian thought that a treaty only gave the white man the right to use the land.

No Indian had ever owned a piece of land. His tribe might claim certain territory for hunting. But it "belonged" to the tribe only as long as the tribe was able to keep other tribes from hunting there. Sioux Indians sneaked into Chippewa woods to kill a deer, and Chippewas roved out onto Sioux prairies to get buffaloes. Both plains tribes and earthlodge people went into the Badlands to catch eagles.

When the white settler died, his children inherited his homestead. When an Indian died, his goods were divided among those in his band who might have greatest need of his goods. Unlike the white man of wealth or class, the Indian's children inherited neither title nor position nor goods. Among Indians, each person through his own deeds must earn his place.

What did the Indian child inherit? Whatever could not be divided. The honor of his family's good reputation. The ways he had been taught as a warrior and hunter. The girl inherited the teachings of her family, the embroidery designs of her clan or tribe.

White soldiers marched in order, following the commands of an officer. The officer told the soldiers to halt, when to fire their guns. To take orders—not to have sense enough to know what to shoot at and when—this seemed stupid to the Indian.

An Indian went with his war chief to attack an enemy tribe. The war party split into small groups when they sighted the enemy. Each warrior decided for himself when it was best to take aim, or how to kill an enemy.

The Indian did not respect white men who talked fast and much. Among the Indians of old times, good manners dictated careful speech. If an Indian were asked a question, he did not answer right away. Thought came before speech. Therefore to show respect to the questioner, one must take time to think out a worthy reply.

The Indian believed that not only did food nourish the body, but so did fresh air and sunshine. He wore as few clothes as possible so sun and air could benefit his body. While the white man considered the Indian uncivilized for wearing no more than a breechcloth, the Indian thought the white man foolish for covering himself from head to foot with tight and clumsy clothes.

In trading with the white man, the Indian soon found his own simple way of life upset. He wanted what the white man could trade him: guns, sharp knives and axes, iron kettles, brightly-colored beads, and blankets. When he had a gun, the Indian held a big advantage over an enemy that could fight only with spear and arrow.

For generations, the Indian had hunted only as many animals as he needed for food, clothing, shelter, and tools. After the white trader's coming, the Indian had to kill more and more animals for furs to barter to the trader. The Indian wife's responsibility had always been to flesh and tan skins. The increasing number of skins she must prepare for the trader now made her almost a slave to the work.

Too often the white trader was out "to make a fast buck," and so he kept increasing the number of skins he wanted for the trade goods the Indian wanted. What was worse, the trader gave the Indian whiskey and rum (usually diluted with water). Under the influence of liquor, the Indian bartered foolishly to the trader's advantage. Once he developed a craving for the "firewater," the Indian came more and more under the influence of the trader.

Coins of money had no meaning to the Indian, nor did the yellow dust and nuggets the white man treasured.

In old times, tribes had traded with one another and in using sign language had exchanged news as well. In the same way, the Indians learned how other tribes had signed treaties with the white man, and the white man had broken his word— usually to get more of the Indian's hunting grounds.

The Indian could not read what the white man wrote on a treaty paper. Unable to keep accounts, he could not prove that the white man cheated him in treaty goods or rations. But the Indian soon concluded that when the white man made a treaty, it was so the white man could get what he wanted.

And so the prairie Indians watched the white man with growing suspicion, and they kept a jealous eye on Uncle Buffalo. They knew how tribe after tribe had lost their hunting grounds to the whites. If they did not drive the white man out of the buffalo country, would the Indian not become as serfs to the white man?

72—Chief Little Crow (T. W. Wood painting)

VII—Warpath

1 - The Sioux Uprising

When Dakota Territory was created, 5,000 Sioux were crowded together on a Minnesota reservation ten miles wide and 150 miles long on the south side of the Minnesota River. Their chiefs had signed a treaty by which the Sioux had given up 28 million acres of land in exchange for $71,000 each year and food provisions.

At the Reservation, the proud Sioux warriors were told they should learn to farm, and earn a living the way white men did. To the hunter who had roamed over vast prairies, farming was woman's work. Only a tenth of the Sioux men tried to farm. Many hunted beyond the Reservation. Because in their own lodges, it had always been their custom to feed any one who entered, they stopped at settler's homes and asked for food—and they helped themselves to garden and field produce.

Far to the south, the white man fought his own white brother in the Civil War. Among the Sioux on the Reservation, rumor claimed that the Negroes had captured the Great White Father's city. Many white soldiers had gone from the northwestern military posts to take part in the Civil War. Unhappy warriors corraled on the Reservation began asking if this was not the time to rise against the whites and win back the Sioux hunting grounds.

In July, 1862, about 800 lodges of Sioux gathered at the Reservation Agency for the scheduled money payment and food rations. The food arrived on time, but the Agent refused to distribute it until the $71,000 gold payment came.

Hungry, resentful, and suspicious that the Agent was cheating them, several hundred warriors surrounded the Agency storehouse on August 4. They fired their guns into the air, and broke into the warehouse to get food.

The Agency soldiers trained artillery on the Indians and cleared them out. Indian Agent Galbraith then gave them a small issue of food which the Indians soon ate.

"When men are hungry, they help themselves," warned Chief Little Crow. "We may take our own way to keep ourselves from starving."

For some time there had been organized among the younger Indian men a soldier society as of olden times. This soldier society wanted to kill all the whites. It had members in every village on the Reservation.

Throughout the night of August 17 these young Indian soldiers gathered chiefs and braves for a council at the brick house of Chief Little Crow. Several of the chiefs said that it would be impossible to drive out the whites. Even when they were accused of being cowards, they still held their stand.

In the darkness outside the house, a growing number of warriors gathered, restlessly waiting for the word to attack.

Little Crow warned that whites were as grasshoppers in number, that the Sioux would die like rabbits hunted by hungry wolves. But he added, "Little Crow is no coward! He will die with you!"

Overhearing this outside, the young warriors thought this meant that Little Crow would lead them in attacking and driving out the whites. So in the darkness of early morning they stole away to begin a week of killing, stealing, and burning. At the Agency that morning they killed nearly every white man. They took the white women and children captive.

All day Monday the Indians scattered to attack the German settlements along the Minnesota River. Terrified survivors ran, spreading word of the killings. Some reached Fort Ridgeley where that very day the gold payment of $71,000 now arrived.

From Fort Ridgeley, young Private William Sturgis rode 165 miles to Fort Snelling to bring word of the outbreak.

The Indians attacked Fort Ridgeley, but refugees and a handful of soldiers successfully defended it.

H. H. Sibley left Fort Snelling with four companies of soldiers. In a battle with the Indians at Birch Coulee, he lost many men, but more soldiers arrived so that at Wood Lake on September 23 the Sibley forces put the Indians on the run. Braves and chiefs now fled to Dakota Territory.

An estimated 400 whites had been killed by the Sioux, and 300 white captives were later freed. Sibley's soldiers rounded up about 2,000 Indians, most of them women and children. Nearly 400 braves were tried in military courts and 306 of them sentenced to be hanged. Through the efforts of Henry Benjamin Whipple, an Episcopalian bishop, President Lincoln reduced the number of condemned to 38. These were hanged at Mankato on December 26, 1862.

Congress in the same month abolished all treaties and land grants and annuities of the Sioux in Minnesota and ordered that the tribe be expelled to a Reservation in Dakota Territory.

2—The Siege of Fort Abercrombie

In August, 1862, Fort Abercrombie had no well, no stockades or bastions. It was only a cluster of four wooden buildings, a small brick storehouse, a saw mill, and stables. River woods to the north and east provided cover for sniping Indians should they come.

A St.Paul grocer, Captain John Vander Horck, had brought 78 volunteers to the fort in March. At the fort they found only 2,000 rounds of shot that would fit their guns. Though Vander Horck had sent back to Fort Snelling for more ammunition, none had arrived on August 20 when word first came of the Sioux uprising.

Vander Horck did not take this news seriously. Not until August 23 did he realize the danger to the people of the Fort Abercrombie area when a messenger arrived from St. Cloud, 152 miles to the east. He brought with him the earliest newspaper accounts of the massacres along the Minnesota River. He also brought orders that Vander Horck should keep at the fort a treaty train of goods bound for the Chippewas in the north.

By this time the uprising had spread as far south in Dakota Territory as Sioux Falls near which two men were killed in a field. Yankton men built stockades with the lumber intended for the new capitol. and the Territorial Officials all fled to Sioux City, Iowa.

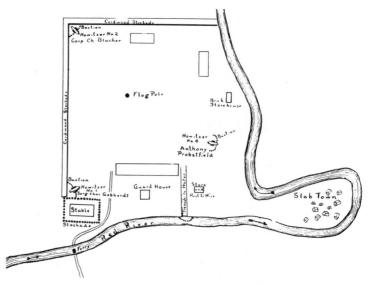

74—A drawing which shows the general plan of Fort Abercrombie at the time of the August-September, 1862, siege

Now Vander Horck sent out messengers to warn settlers along the river. Civilians straggled into the fort, bringing their cattle and horses with them. Walter Hills and another man volunteered to ride to Fort Snelling to ask for more soldiers and ammunition.

While word came of men killed in the Breckenridge area, soldiers and civilians worked desperately in building a stockade of cordwood, logs, and sod mixed with barrels of pork, corned beef and flour. They dug fortifications.

On August 30 a large band of Indians stampeded the cattle, horses, and Government mules grazing to the west of the fort. Before dawn, September 3, Vander Horck went out to inspect sentry as usual. A sentinel, nervous after sighting a skulking Indian, accidentally shot the captain in the arm. While the surgeon bandaged Vander Horck's wound, Indians began a two-hour attack, sniping from the woods. They set fire to the hay stacks, wounded three soldiers, and got away with four horses.

On September 5 Walter Hills returned from Snelling and said more soldiers and ammunition would come. The next day Indians again fired from the woods, killing one man and wounding two others. Fearful that a great number of Indians would surround them, the fort defenders built a breastwork 8 feet high around the barracks.

While sentries stood guard every hour, day followed day without attack. When no more soldiers had come by September 23, Hills and three other men volunteered to go back to Fort Snelling again and beg for help. An escort of 30 men took Hills through the timber. But a mile from Fort Abercrombie, Indians ambushed and killed two of the escort.

Suddenly a cloud of dust appeared southeast of the fort. Smoke from a grass fire billowed in the same direction. It separated fleeing Indians from 350 soldiers who were finally arriving.

73—Stampede of frightened Territorial officials (Armstrong)

Four days later, soldiers escorted 60 men, women, and children safely to St. Cloud. With the siege over, the soldiers cut down all the timber and brush along the river. They constructed three blockhouses and a palisade which would never have to serve in defense.

3 - *Paleface Revenge*

The horror of the Minnesota Massacre shocked all Americans. Because trained soldiers were already engaged in the Civil War, any expedition to punish the Sioux would have to be made up of volunteers.

In southeastern Dakota Territory, many people abandoned their farms. At Yankton, residents voted whether to run or to fight. Most decided to stay and fight. Fifty men worked with spades, axes, and teams to build breastworks around a five-acre tract of buildings. Here families collected, expecting each night to be attacked by the Sioux. When days passed with no sign of Indians, farmers began returning to their fields and livestock.

A local militia organized while citizens at Vermillion, Yankton, and Bon Homme appealed for military protection. But the nearest soldiers remained at Sioux City, Iowa, where the Government officials had gone.

That their Government officers had deserted them angered the settlers. Then President Lincoln ordered that only if the officials returned to Yankton and stayed there would they be paid their salaries.

Yankton men built a two-story capitol building and here the Territorial Assembly met in December, 1862. A rough-and-tumble session began but soon settled down for serious law-making.

By midwinter word came to the Dakotans that an expedition was being organized against the hostile Sioux. Dakota Cavalry arrived in May and began patrolling the settlements, and farmers dared plant their fields.

Yankton's brass band welcomed General Alfred H. Sully's army to the capital city. Territory residents cheered themselves hoarse as they watched the army train of 234 wagons, 400 cattle, 320 mules and 2,118 horses and 2,500 fighting men paraded into their settlement.

This Sully Expedition planned to go up the Missouri in four steamboats. Another force led by H. H. Sibley from Fort Snelling would come through eastern Dakota and drive the Indians westward. Sully would come up the Missouri and with Sibley surround the Sioux.

4 - *The Sibley Expedition*

With 3,500 men and a 225-mule wagon train, Sibley set out for Dakota on June 16, 1863, to hunt down Little Crow and his warriors. A cautious leader acquainted with Indian ways, Sibley required his men to dig shallow trenches for their protection whenever they made camp.

Bugle call sounded two and three in the morning, with breakfast at four, and marching until noon. During the afternoons, the large beef herd and the horses and mules grazed, and teamsters gathered hay which the animals could eat after they corraled for the night.

On June 24, the expedition entered Dakota Territory near Big Stone Lake. They made their first camp on North Dakota soil, July 2, at Lake Tewaukon where the men went swimming after a day of stifling heat and dust.

Day after day they plodded on through high temperatures and over prairies so parched that the ground lay cracked. Men often fainted and some became sick from the heat. Grasshoppers left little grass for the animals.

On their way to Camp Buel, cavalrymen rode into Fish Lake and hooked pickerel with their sabers. By now men had accustomed themselves to another daily chore—gathering dried buffalo manure for their cooks' camp fires.

75—General Henry Hastings Sibley

On the Fourth of July, Sibley's army camped by the Sheyenne River. They fired 39 volleys to salute the states and territories, and they heard some patriotic speeches. While they rested here, where grass was more plentiful, mail and a supply train arrived from Fort Abercrombie.

On July 11, they again went on the march, making their next major stop at Camp Atchinson by Lake Jessie. Here they dug breastworks, stored surplus supplies, and left several soldiers to guard sick men and beasts.

The army continued westward and met a large company of Pembina Hunters near Hawk's Nest Hill. The priest with these Metis people had with him a white boy he had ransomed from the fleeing Sioux. A large number of such Indians, Sibley was told, were but a few days' travel ahead.

On July 24 the expedition sighted a band of about 2,000 Indians encamped on the top and gullied sides of a rocky hill near a lake. Halfbreed army scouts in civilian clothes rode out to meet a small group of Indians coming from their camp. Young Dr. Josiah S. Weiser, in army uniform, noticed this, and since he could speak Sioux, he also went out to meet the Indians. He had just given some tobacco and hardtack to a few of them when an Indian shot him dead.

At sight of their fallen comrade, soldiers charged after the Indians who now galloped past the troops, shooting from under the necks of their horses. Suddenly, a thunderstorm broke over the battle. Lightning struck the saber from Colonel Samuel McPhail's hand and killed Private John Murphy. For about 15 miles westward, the Sibley forces pursued the warriors, killing a number of them. The Indians failed to shoot any of the soldiers.

On July 26 the Sibley army again encountered Indians in large numbers at Dead Buffalo Lake. Cannon kept the red men at a distance.

At Stony Lake, General Sibley watched Indians assembling in a larger number than ever before. Warriors on horses rode out to form a line several miles wide in front of the army camp.

Sibley led his men straight toward the warriors. Right away the wide band of mounted Indians disappeared over the horizon.

The fleeing Indians reached the Missouri River near what is now known as Sibley Island. By the time the soldiers reached the place, the Indians had gotten safely across in bullboats and hastily-made rafts. But behind them they had to leave camp equipment, fresh buffalo hides, tallow, and pemmican. All this, and more than a hundred carts and wagons belonging to the Indians, Sibley's men burned.

Sibley's Expedition should have been at the river to stop the fleeing Indians. Sibley waited in camp for two days, firing cannon occasionally in the daytime and rockets at night to signal for Sully.

On August 1, Sibley gave up trying to connect with the other expedition and started back for

Minnesota, returning by way of Fort Abercrombie. Indians had killed or mortally wounded ten of Sibley's men; thirteen soldiers had died of illness. Soldiers who had killed an estimated 150 Indians could not know whether or not their victims had taken part in the Minnesota Massacre.

But Sibley's men came back to tell friends and relatives of a great and grassy land. Dry it was in that terrible drouth, but with rain it could pasture thousands and thousands of cattle. On these prairies, fields could be planted to grain without the hard labor of first clearing trees away.

5 - Sully's Expedition of 1863

General Alfred Sully could hardly be blamed for not hearing the cannon Sibley had fired at Apple Creek near the Missouri. Even two weeks after Sibley had left the Missouri, Sully was 160 miles down the river.

From the start, unusually low water had slowed his supply steamers. Soldiers walking along the shore had to wait for the steamers to struggle past sandbars and snags. After deciding he could get the boats no farther, Sully left the steamers at Fort Pierre.

Then his army struck northward, marching along the east side of the Missouri. Hot, dusty winds poured over them. But they hurried on, taking no time for digging night-time trenches.

76—General Alfred Sully

On August 28, the men at the front sighted Long Lake and broke ranks for the water. While the men slaked their thirst, a scout brought a limping old Indian to General Sully. From this wounded Sioux, Sully learned that Sibley had gone back to Minnesota, and the Indians had also gone eastward to the James River. Now the Expedition headed in the same direction.

On September 3, an advance battalion sighted an Indian camp of several hundred lodges. At that time, General Sully was ten miles behind the battalion.

Several chiefs, carrying a white flag, came out to talk with Major E. A. House, the commander of the advance battalion. While this was going on, the expedition cavalry and eight cannon rushed toward the Indian camp in case House's battalion might be attacked. When Sully arrived, Indian women were hastily packing for flight. Darkness, soon coming, would help that flight.

Sully's battalions nearly surrounded the Indian camp. Shots suddenly turned the great camp into a wild babble of shrieks and war whoops. A great number of Indians waved buffalo robes to frighten the cavalry horses so their riders could not manage them. This accomplished, the Indians broke through and ran down a ravine. But the soldiers on higher ground fired at the fleeing Indians, killing men, women, and children.

In the gathering darkness, Indians ran in every direction. When night fell, bugles called the soldiers back to the hill where a fire served as a beacon.

Morning brought terrible labor. From the prairies about Whitestone Hill, the soldiers brought 36 of their own wounded, and the bodies of 20 dead to bury upon the hill. They counted about 200 Indians killed and estimated that as many may have been wounded.

The soldiers found little Indian babies, too. They brought these babies to the 130 Indians held prisoners.

Then the soldiers piled and burned the great stores of buffalo meat, provisions, and equipment. Buffalo fat ran in streams down the burning heaps.

A few days after leaving the scene of battle, Sully met a band of friendly Indians and gave them the rest of the orphaned babies. Then he returned to his moored boats and went down the Missouri to Sioux City, Iowa.

Where once had been a favorite buffalo ground, a monument now stands on Whitestone Hill to commemorate the bloody battle. No more would the Sioux have dominion over the prairies east of the Missouri River.

77—Whitestone Hill monument

6 - Sully's Northwestern Expedition of 1864

In the spring of 1864, Sully led a third expedition against the Sioux. While this army marched up the east side of the Missouri, steamers carried their provisions and equipment up the river to where Fort Rice would be built.

At this place, the steamers ferried the soldiers across the river. Colonel David J. Hill stayed behind with six companies of men to build the fort from cottonwood logs. Sully then started for the Cannonball River country where they expected to find the Sioux.

The Expedition going along the Cannonball consisted of 2,200 cavalry and mounted infantry, two companies of battery, two companies of road builders, 400 freight wagons, 70 Indian guides, and a beef herd. Six hundred emigrants heading for the Idaho gold fields had come along.

Meanwhile three steamers carried army supplies up the Missouri to meet the Expedition on the Yellowstone River.

For several days, the soldiers traveled westward. Clouds of grasshoppers left little grass for mules, horses, and beef stock. Drouth and heat again plagued the army.

A week after leaving Fort Rice, scouts reported a great encampment of Sioux just south of the Killdeer Mountains. Sully decided to head directly there. First, he ordered a corral of the heavier emigrant wagons, and inside this corral the goldseeker families set up camp.

Leaving a contingent of soldiers to guard the goldseekers, Sully set out after the Sioux. The third morning after leaving the emigrant camp, Sully saw thousands of Indians coming toward him across a level plain. He formed his troops into a hollow square and waited. As they drew closer, the long lines of braves began circling about the square of soldiers. The Indians rushed for the whites, their war cries echoing over the sun-scorched prairies.

When the Indians came within 600 feet, the soldiers opened fire. There followed a bloody battle that wore on all day under the hot sun. Up the steep sides of the Mountain Where We Kill Deer, the Indian women and children fled, their warriors fighting to protect them from the oncoming whites. When night fell, the Indians had disappeared into the darkness, over the Killdeer Mountains and into the breaks beyond. Cavalrymen surrounded one butte on top of which a band of warriors stood their ground.

The soldiers decided they would wait until morning, then climb the butte and kill the Indians.

Dawn came. The soldiers climbed warily up the butte, expecting arrows and gunfire. On the summit they found not one warrior, but there was a strange hole with wind coming up out of it.

78A—**View from top of Killdeer Mountains** (Russell Reid photo)

All next day, the soldiers burned what was left of the 1,600 lodges, great heaps of buffalo meat, dried berries, fresh and tanned hides, travois, and clothing. They buried five of their own men in unmarked graves. Thirty times that number of Indians lay dead over the miles of battleground. Then the Expedition returned to the emigrant camp, and Sully ordered the march west. The second afternoon of marching, they reached the Badlands at a place believed to be the Painted Canyon. How could they cross the Badlands and then reach the Yellowstone where the steamers were to meet them with supplies?

But one of the guides said he knew this Place Where the Hills Look at Each Other. He could find a pass through.

He led the Expedition southward, and the men camped at a place now known as Sully Springs. All that night, dogs and coyotes howled from the surrounding buttes, and Indians called from high cliffs, "Sleep well this night, you dog-faced white men! Tomorrow you will die!"

The next day the guide led the army to the floor of the Little Missouri River valley. Sometimes they had to dig a roadway into the steep bank of a clay-walled hill. At times soft earth gave way, and heavy wagons rolled down into a ravine. Yet they reached the bottomlands and camped beside fresh water and grasshopper-infested grass.

Early one morning the Expedition started single-file up ravines that would lead them out of the valley and up to the plains northwest to the Yellowstone.

Now thousands of hostile Indians gathered to avenge their losses at Killdeer Mountain. They sneaked up ravines, hid behind boulders, climbed to the tops of buttes, trying to ambush a part of the train which now stretched three and four miles.

Mules pulled the heavy freight wagons, and oxen the emigrant wagons inside of which women and

78—**Medicine Hole on top of Killdeer Mountain** (Sheldon Green photo)

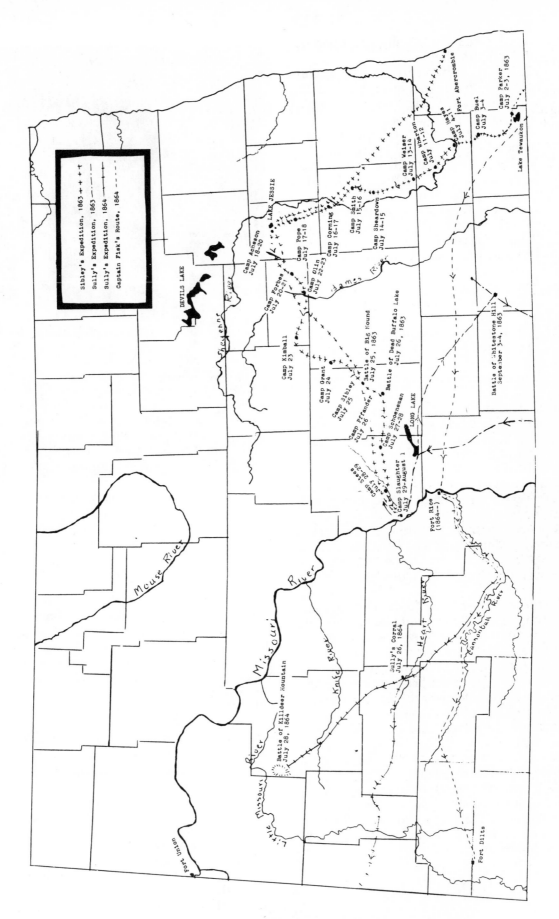

**79—Routes followed by the Sibley and Sully Expeditions,
and by the Fisk wagon train (Author)**

children cowered. General Sully lay sick upon the jolting bed of a military wagon.

Again and again the cannon fired to clear Indians from the buttes on both sides of the narrow, winding trail. Late in the afternoon, the first wagons straggled out upon the prairies above the breaks.

At last, on August 8, the entire Expedition was out of the Badlands and camped for the night at what is known as Sully's Water Hole. All through the night, Indians hid upon Cone Butte and fired in the direction of the white men.

The next day, the Expedition started past Flat Top Butte and the Indians tried desperately to stop the train. Again the cannon stopped them, and afterwards the warriors scattered, trying no longer to attack the whites.

Worried over lack of water and feed for their animals, the Expedition traveled 32 miles on August 11. They trudged through a prairie made into a desert by grasshoppers and drouth. Oxen, mules, and horses, weakened from lack of water and feed, stumbled and fell, unable to get up again. Soldiers shot more than a hundred beasts dead to end their suffering.

On the afternoon of August 12, the weary train caught sight of the Yellowstone River bluffs. When they neared the river, men ran like a herd of cattle to fling themselves down on the river bank or to dive into the water to slake their thirst and cool their bodies. When they reached camp that night, they had to cut cottonwood branches to feed their horses because grass was so scarce.

Two steamers waited. The third had struck a snag below Fort Union and had sunk with all its cargo. The two steamers ferried the Expedition to the west side of the river. The goldseekers went on their way.

The steamers now started down river, the soldiers marching alongside by land. After reaching Fort Union on August 18, Sully selected the site for a new army post, Fort Buford.

At Fort Berthold, he left a company of cavalry to protect the three earthlodge tribes from the warring Sioux. A short distance from Fort Rice, messengers informed him that a band of goldseekers were under Indian attack on the edge of the Badlands, about 160 miles west of Fort Rice. Sully dispatched Colonel Dill with 550 infantry, 300 cavalry, and a section of artillery to the rescue.

Then he divided the remainder of his Expedition, some going eastward across the prairie to winter near Lake Traverse, the rest to go down the Missouri. And so ended the white man's efforts to avenge the Minnesota Massacre.

80—Captain James L. Fisk

7 - The Goldseekers

For men who lived in the Midwest, the nearest route to the Montana and Idaho gold strikes lay across the Dakota prairies where the angry Sioux ranged.

A nation struggling with civil war welcomed the gold discoveries. Secretary of War Edwin Stanton appointed young Captain James L. Fisk to provide military escort for American goldseekers wanting to cross Dakota Territory by wagon train.

In 1862 a party of 80 emigrants left Minnesota, went to Pembina, and then west to Montana in order to avoid the Sioux. In escorting his first train of gold-seeking emigrants that same year, Fisk successfully followed the more southerly route taken by Governor Stevens on his railway survey in 1853. The following year Fisk led the goldseekers along the route followed by General Sibley, and then on to Montana without any attack from Indians.

In 1864, Fisk wanted to shorten his route even more. With 50 cavalrymen to protect the emigrants, he traveled for a month across the prairies until he reached the Missouri directly across from Fort Rice. Here the party waited for a week until a steamer came along and ferried them over the river.

At Fort Rice, Fisk learned that General Sully had successfully fought the Indians at Killdeer Mountain. So he reasoned that it would be safe to travel directly west over unfamiliar prairies.

With 140 men, 7 women and 12 children in 80 wagons and carts, Fisk left Fort Rice on August 23. A corps of 47 cavalrymen went along.

Fisk followed Sully's trail until it turned northwest. Not an Indian had been spied since they left the fort. So the guns lay packed away in the wagons.

At Deep Creek which had a dry bed but steep banks, the teamsters had to dig a pass. All the wagons crossed without trouble except the last one which was heavily loaded with drug supplies and whiskey.

It tipped over in the soft earth. An extra wagon containing 5,000 rounds of ammunition and seven guns stayed behind with several soldiers to get the wagon righted. The rest of the party continued on.

When the wagon train had gotten about a mile from Deep Creek, a band of Sioux swooped down from a butte to attack the two wagons. At sound of the shooting, the wagon train ahead formed a corral. Cavalrymen and teamsters raced back.

The Indians scurried for the breaks, leaving the two wagons looted and on fire, eight men dead and several wounded.

Jefferson Dilts, an old trapper who served as a guide, had been scouting ahead, and rode directly into the scalp-happy Indians. He emptied his revolver at them, killing six warriors. He reached the emigrant train with three arrows sticking in his back.

A furious storm raged as the men carried the dead and wounded to the corral. On low ground it was not long before the camp flooded. Through the long night, men stood ready with rifles for an enemy that did not come.

The train went on its way the next morning. But Indians made running attacks. Though gunshots spattered wagon sides, not one emigrant was killed. Several Indians fell under the shooting of soldiers and the wounded Jefferson Dilts.

The party continued ten miles. Indians kept appearing on hills and buttes, some of them intoxicated from the whiskey supplies of the drug store wagon.

When the goldseekers reached the edge of the Badlands, Fisk realized they could not cross through where Indians could ambush them from the steep hills and buttes. They must get help from Fort Rice before they dared go any farther.

He found a level piece of ground near a spring of water. Here they would build a sod fort to protect themselves until Fort Rice soldiers could rescue them.

After driving off a small number of attacking Indians from a nearby butte, men hitched oxen to plows and cut sod into strips. Men and women built the sod strips into a wall six feet high and two feet thick around the entire corral.

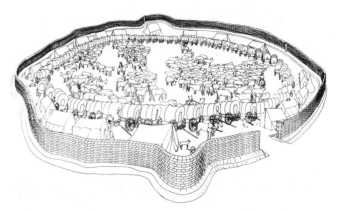

81—Drawing showing the general plan of Fort Dilts

The night of September 5, eleven men volunteered to sneak out of the fort and ride to Fort Rice for help. The following day, seven of them returned after losing their way. One man was killed by Indians.

The Indians again attacked the encampment, but were driven off. Jefferson Dilts and two soldiers died and were buried under the wall of the fort.

Next the Indians appeared on a small hill. There they set up a small flag of truce and went away. On the flag stick, Captain Fisk found a note written on wrapping paper. It was written by Mrs. Fanny Kelly who had been captured by the Indians on July 12. She begged to be freed.

Other notes followed. The Indians wanted ammunition and other weapons. Fisk offered them three good horses, some flour, sugar, coffee, and a load of supplies in exchange for Mrs. Kelly. The Indians would not give her up.

When Colonel Dill and his men came to release them, the women joyfully baked bread and doughnuts for everyone to celebrate the end of sixteen days in the sod-walled fort.

The emigrant train returned to Fort Rice. From there most of them returned to their old homes.

The following year, Captain Fisk, without military escort, led his fourth train of 160 wagons safely to Montana by way of Fort Union. He retired from the Army in 1865.

Other wagon trains followed the same route across Dakota Territory. One, in 1868, after leaving Fort Buford, was met by threatening Indians. The whites hastily assembled their brass band to play "Yankee Doodle." This so charmed the Indians that they let the emigrants go marching on their way, stepping lively to:

Yankee Doodle, keep it up! Yankee Doodle Dandy! Mind the music and the step and with the girls be handy!

And what of Fanny Kelly? She gained her freedom in early December when an Indian, Crawler, exchanged her for clothing and supplies at Fort Sully. Congress voted her a reward of $5,000 for her efforts to save Fort Sully from attack. Her book, **My Captivity among the Sioux**, was a best-seller for many years.

VIII - Dakota Beginnings

1 - Early Struggles

During the early years of Dakota Territory, drouth and grasshoppers discouraged farming. To most Americans the Territory remained a part of "The Great American Desert." So it did not appeal to landseekers looking for a place in which to farm and live.

Government officials continued to be appointed by the President of the United States. Persons who lived in Dakota were seldom placed in such offices. Many of the outsiders who came to serve as officials used their offices to get money they did not earn.

Especially after the Sioux Uprising, white men in Dakota Territory did not look favorably upon Indians. An increasing number of Indians were sent to live on Reservations in Dakota Territory. White Indian agents put in charge of such Reservations found it easy to cheat the Indian who could neither read nor write. For Dakota farmers, the Reservations provided the best market for the grain and meat they were able to grow.

Separate treaties were made with nine groups of Sioux in 1865, and the following year with other tribes in northern Dakota. As a result, about 16,000 more Sioux came in on Reservations. The Laramie Treaty of 1868 promised the Sioux control of what was called the Great Sioux Reservation.

This covered, in Dakota Territory, the entire country west of the Missouri River up to the 46th parallel.

When the rains came and the grasshoppers withdrew, a period of good crops lasted into the Seventies. More and more people began to believe that Dakota Territory could become farmland, particularly if a railway would be built to reach eastern markets.

One of the earliest ways of getting people to come to live in Dakota Territory was the townsite company. A townsite company would try to decide where a town would likely be established. Then when they had decided on such a site, they would buy the land. There might not be a single building where such a town was planned. All the plans were on paper—with streets and avenues laid out and this "paper town" was divided into town lots. Then they would try to sell the lots and interest people to build there. Some townsite companies tried sincerely to establish towns that would prosper; others tried only to fool people into buying lots.

The first such towns were planned at likely river landing places or where water could be used for mills. Later, when railways were expected, the paper towns were located where the railroad might come and an agricultural center could develop.

83—Pioneer Dakota farmers fighting grasshoppers (Frank Leslie's Illustrated Newspaper, 1888)

2 - Army Outposts

Among the Sioux, bitter feelings continued toward the whites. This mighty tribe saw their land, their buffalo, and their way of life being taken from them. The Sibley and Sully Expeditions had further angered them.

They sniped at river boats on the Missouri. They killed a third of the woodhawks who cut firewood for river steamers.

For generations, the Sioux had persecuted the earthlodge Indians along the upper Missouri. These

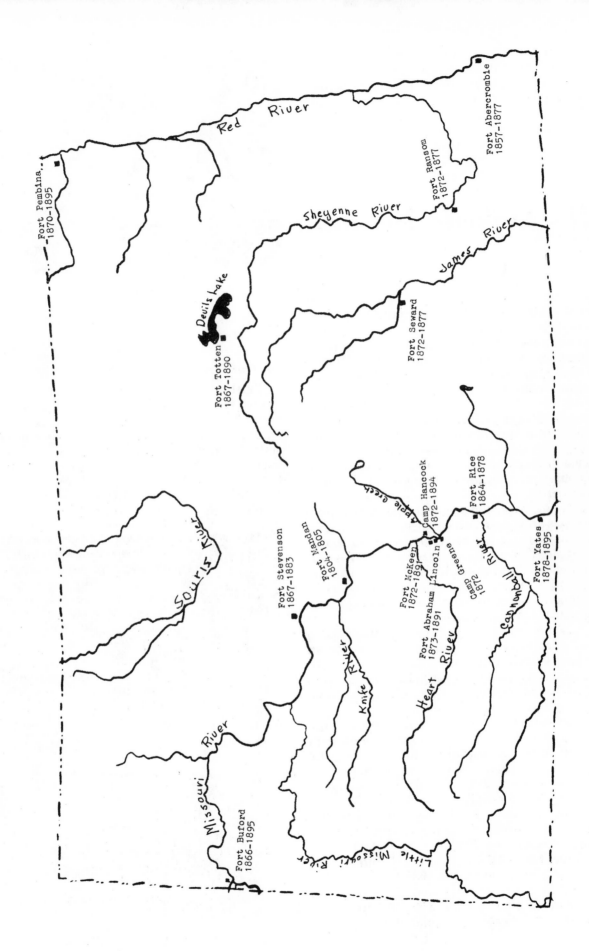

84—Military posts in North Dakota area (Author)

The following labels appear on the map:

- Red River
- Fort Pembina 1870-1895
- Sheyenne River
- Fort Ransom 1872-1877
- Fort Abercrombie 1857-1877
- James River
- Devils Lake
- Fort Seward 1872-1877
- Fort Totten 1867-1890
- Souris River
- Apple Creek
- Camp Hancock 1872-1894
- Fort Rice 1864-1878
- Fort Stevenson 1867-1883
- Fort Mandan 1804-1805
- Fort McKeen 1872-1891
- Fort Abraham Lincoln 1873-1891
- Camp Greene 1872
- Cannonball River
- Fort Yates 1878-1895
- Knife River
- Heart River
- Missouri River
- Fort Buford 1866-1895
- Little Missouri River

tribes begged the Great White Father to send white soldiers to defend them against the Sioux.

And so soldiers began building military posts in the upper Missouri country. Sully's soldiers built Fort Rice, the first such military post west of Fort Abercrombie. Indians attacked the builders, and soldiers lost their lives while cutting cottonwood timbers, or guarding other workers.

They built this Fort Rice on a level spot about 100 feet above the Missouri. The buildings, the high palisades surrounding them, the bastions on the southwest and northeast corners were all made of cottonwood logs.

When the cottonwood logs dried, they shrank and warped. This caused cracks in the walls. Dust and snow blew in. Rats, mice, and insects, sometimes even rattlesnakes, got inside. Rats destroyed so much grain needed by horses that few horses could be kept at the fort.

The sodroofed log buildings soon began to rot and crumble. So the fort had to be rebuilt. It was abandoned in 1878 when another stronger fort (Yates) was built nearby.

Where the Yellowstone and Missouri Rivers join, soldiers built Fort Buford in 1866. Some of the building material came from the Fort Union fur trading post which no longer operated. Soldiers stationed at Fort Buford were to guard against the Assiniboin, Cree, Hidatsa, and Sioux who roamed that region.

Another army post was established not far from where Lewis and Clark had built their Fort Mandan. Soldiers stationed there were to protect the earth-lodge people. At first, this Fort Stevenson was only a cluster of tents and makeshift sheds. The soldiers built sod huts and crude cottonwood shelters. Their first winter at Fort Stevenson was so cold that some of their cattle froze to death.

At Fort Stevenson, river steamers unloaded a saw mill, artillery, arms and ammunition for an inland fort. Ox teams freighted this equipment 126 miles to the south side of Devils Lake. Here soldiers built Fort Totten of crude buildings to shelter them the first winter.

Soldiers established trails between forts for the mail carriers and freighters. To keep the carriers from losing their way over the trackless prairies, the soldiers marked much of the trail with piles of stones. Dugouts, sod huts, and log cabins along the way provided shelter from storms. At such stopping places, a hardy frontiersman stayed to care for the horses that riders and freighters would exchange. A trail went west from Fort Abercrombie to Fort Ransom (built in 1867), north to Fort Totten, then west to Fort Stevenson on the Missouri.

Meanwhile, early settlers had discovered the fertile soil of the Red River Valley and hopes were growing that a railway might come that way.

85—Fort Totten

3 - The First Farmer

Charles Bottineau came to the Walhalla country as a fur trader in 1859. When he found how fertile the soil was, he began farming soon after. He built himself a large log house and brought in several Metis to work for him on his farm. By the time Rolette filed the first homestead entry in 1868, Bottineau had a hundred acres of grain growing. He also continued with the fur business and became quite wealthy.

86—Charles Bottineau

He raised his first crops for food and for livestock feed. Then he hauled wheat to the Selkirk settlement in Canada. He raised cattle and supplied Kittson and Rolette with oxen for their Red River Cartways, and he operated a line of carts himself. When Fort Pembina was built in 1870. Bottineau suppled the soldiers with beef.

His wheat crops sometimes yielded 40 bushels to the acre. His men cut the grain with cradle scythes, and threshed it by hand.

Around home Farmer Bottineau dressed in buckskins, but when he visited St. Paul or Winnipeg, he wore a stylish suit and silk hat. And he loaned money to a friend of his by the name of James J. Hill.

87—Early Northern Pacific train

4 - The First Homesteaders

In 1869, several families settled in the Hickson area in what is now Cass County. A few years later, other settlers came on foot, driving cows along with their ox-drawn wagons. They began the first home building along the Goose River. Others soon followed, rejoicing in the free Red River land.

They bought supplies at two Hudson's Bay Company trading posts at Frog Point and Caledonia. These settlers harvested their first crops by hand. Later they used a horse-powered threshing machine loaned to them by the Hudson's Bay Company.

One of them was so enthusiastic about farming in the Red River Valley that he wrote a rhyme and sent it back to his friends in the East:

If by thieves and doctors bled
Half your cash and blood has fled,
Gather up your stove and bed
And settle on the Goose.
Though Adam took his wife's advice
And got expelled from Paradise,
You'll find another just as nice
By squatting on the Goose.

5 - The Iron Trail

Congress gave both money and land grants to the Union Pacific and Central Pacific lines so they could build the first railroad across the United States. This southern railway extended from Omaha to San Francisco.

So that a northern railway could be built from Lake Superior to Puget Sound, Congress provided generous grants of land to the railroad builders. President Abraham Lincoln signed the law which then gave alternate sections of land 40 miles on either side of the route through Dakota Territory. This amounted to 10,700,279 acres in what is now North Dakota. Similar land grants were given in other territories which the railway would cross.

In this largest land grant in the history of American railroad building, the company would have right of way across Indian lands. But this did not give whites the right to settle on such Indian lands.

From the sale of this land, the company would get money for the construction of the railway. Such railway land first sold for $2.50 an acre with a 25 percent discount on land cultivated within two years.

The first Northern Pacific construction began in Minnesota in 1870. It reached the Red River on December 12, 1871.

During the winter, a bridge was built across the river. On June 6, 1872, ladies from Fargo on the Prairie took the ferry to Moorhead where they boarded the first locomotive into North Dakota. Garlanded with wild flowers the ladies had gathered, the locomotive chuff-chuffed over the bridge, its whistle blasting three times.

By this time, grading for the railway was done nearly as far as the Jamestown area. Men with spades and horse- or mule-drawn scrapers did all the work. Grading crews lived in tents and worked many miles ahead of the track-laying crew. Like the surveyors, these workers needed soldier protection from Indians.

The track-layers progressed westward at about three miles a day. Winter came early and harshly with only 30 miles of railway unfinished to the Missouri River. Work continued in the spring, and almost everyone in the little town of Edwinton (later called Bismarck) met the first train at Apple Creek, June 5, 1873.

But this was as far as the rails would go for several years. For in the depression of 1873, the Northern Pacific Railway Company went bankrupt.

That same year Congress passed the Timber Culture Act. It allowed settlers to obtain 160 acres

88—The main street of Bismarck, 1873

89—Northern Pacific train crossing Missouri by ferry

90—Testing the new railway bridge across the Missouri

by planting ten acres of it to trees. At the end of eight years, the settler had to have at least 675 trees growing. Such land could be next to a man's homestead. Many groves of tall trees in the Red River Valley today are evidence of such tree claims.

Several wealthy men had invested heavily in the Northern Pacific. Now they decided they would exchange the Northern Pacific bonds for land in the Red River Valley. They would prove to the nation that men could make good money farming in Dakota. They hired men to farm their land. The farms produced wonderful crops. This brought more people to buy NP lands. So the railway company was able to reorganize in 1879 and continue building west of the Missouri River.

Building materials came by rail to Bismarck and during the summer months were ferried across the Missouri. In winter and early spring, tracks laid on the river ice bridged the river. Locomotives puffed across, shuttling back and forth, bringing trainloads of material until the ice began to thaw. This was done until 1883 when the railway bridge was completed.

When the railway reached Sentinel Butte on November 10, 1880, a silver spike was driven into the rail because at that time Sentinel Butte was believed to mark the boundary between Dakota and Montana. The border was actually crossed in 1881.

The NP bridge at Bismarck stands where the buffalo had forded Grandmother River for centuries past. It stood high enough to allow river steamers to pass under it. But the railway would bring an end to riverboat business.

6 - Bonanza Farms

George W. Cass, the Northern Pacific Railway Company president, and Benjamin F. Cheney, a director, were the first to exchange railway bonds for land in the Red River Valley. To manage their lands, they hired Oliver Dalrymple who had been overseeing the largest wheat farm in Minnesota.

By the fall of 1875, Dalrymple had 1,280 acres of land ready for spring seeding. The first harvest in the autumn of 1876 yielded a bonanza harvest of 32,000 bushels of wheat. The profit earned on that first crop caused other bondholders to exchange bonds for land in this new "Nile Valley of the American Continent." In just a few years, several "bonanza farms" were operating.

Since the government land grant had given alternate sections of land to the railway company, the bonanza farms followed a checkerboard pattern of land sections. As the farms developed, most of them divided into five and six thousand acre units supervised by a man responsible to the general farm manager.

On a 5,000-acre subdivision farm, a dozen men cared for the stock and equipment through the winter. Toward spring the supervisor hired ten men to clean and prepare seed. Seeding required about 55 men to harrow the soil. Then they sowed with 8-foot broadcast seeders, and followed this with harrowing again. With spring's work done, 40 men put up hay for the horses and mules and broke more sod until the middle of July.

About 115 men worked in the harvest fields. A dozen or more binders pulled into a field, one behind the other. The wheat shockers followed, setting the bundles upright to dry for threshing. Steam rig threshing crews numbered up to 30 men. Powered by straw-burning engines, these rigs threshed between 850 to 1,000 bushels a day. Straw piles were burned right away, only a small amount of straw being saved for barn litter.

The dozens of huge bonanza farms enjoyed advantages over small farms operated by one man and his family. Because the bonanza farm managers bought in large quantities, they could get lumber at wholesale prices. When a bonanza farm manager bought 75 to 100 head of mules and horses, groceries by the ton, he bought at a discount. When the Grandin Farms bought 38 plows, 35 sets of harnesses, 17 seeders, 27 binders, 32 wagons, and five threshing machines at one time, it cost a third less than what a small farmer would pay. And because the bonanza farms shipped large amounts of grain at one time, it cost them less.

Newspaper reporters and American sightseers brought much favorable publicity to the bonanza farms. No longer was Dakota Territory considered a part of the Great American Desert.

But dry years came and the financial panic of 1893 brought a gradual end to the bonanza farms. All work on bonanza farms was hired. Few of the Easterners who had invested in such farms ever lived on them.

The homesteader who lived on his land and cared for it himself survived. Many of the homesteaders had worked on the bonanza farms to earn money to start their own small farms. During harvest times on the big "wheat factories," men earned a top wage of $2.50 a day.

Actually, the total number of acres operated by bonanza farmers was much less than that by small farm owners.

7 - Exit for Uncle Buffalo

The Spanish, French, and British traders who first came into the Missouri country did not come for buffalo robes. They wanted the finer fur of the beaver. Not until American traders came was there a market for the buffalo robe.

91—Harvesting on a bonanza farm (Independent Farmer and Fireside Companion, November 1, 1870)

92—Shipping grain and lumber on the Red River (Northwest Magazine, March, 1886)

The railroads brought the real danger to the buffalo. Hunters traveled with railway construction crews to supply workers with fresh meat, and most of this came from the buffalo.

As soon as tracks had been laid, the train supplied transportation for thousands of buffalo robes and some buffalo meat to the Eastern markets. Many hundreds of "sportsmen" rode out on new rail spurs to shoot buffalo from the comfort of a coach or an observation car.

After a method was learned for making leather from its hide, the buffalo was shot in even greater numbers. A raw buffalo cow hide on the western Dakota prairies would bring the hunter $3.50 each, and he could sell the meat at 3 and 4 cents a pound. He generally earned $5 for every wild cow he killed. Bulls, yearlings, and calves brought lower prices.

Since the Union Pacific railway was completed first, the buffalo first disappeared from the Southwest. Then hunters entered the Northwest in 1879, following the Northern Pacific. By 1882 about five thousand buffalo hunters and skinners scattered

93—Buffalo "stand." (J. B. Moser painting)

over the northern range. Easterners killed the buffalo just to get a buffalo head trophy and also left thousands of buffaloes dead and unskinned upon the prairies.

The professional hunter who wanted to make money by selling the hides tried to shoot a number of buffaloes at one time. He did this by the "stand" method.

After finding a herd, this hunter walked carefully toward the buffaloes against the wind. He would find a place out of sight of the animals—about 50 or 150 yards from them. Since the herd neither saw, smelled, nor heard the hunter, the beasts kept grazing while the man kept shooting down as many as he could skin.

The hunter usually had one or two men hired to skin for him. A good skinner could handle up to 50 carcasses a day if the animals had been shot close together. After cutting the skin, the skinner used a team of horses to pull the skin off the buffalo body.

The hide shipments on trains told the story of Uncle Buffalo's disappearing from the prairies. In the years when Bismarck served as the western end of the Northern Pacific, some 50,000 buffalo robes arrived there each year by river steamer to be shipped east by rail. After buffalo hides were being made into leather, 75,000 skins came down river to Bismarck in 1881. The next year the Northern Pacific railway carried 200,000 robes and hides to Eastern markets. Three years later such shipments stopped, for Uncle Buffalo had been slaughtered almost to extermination. And his bones lay strewn over the plains.

8 - Dakota Cowpunching

In Dakota Territory, military forts needed herds of cattle to feed the soldiers. Farmers in Minnesota, Iowa, and Dakota Territory drove cattle to the military forts and to Indian Reservations.

As more railways were built, beef could be shipped to the big cities in the East. Men working in western gold mines offered high prices for beef. While early railway construction crews had depended on buffaloes and other wild animals for meat, the men preferred the meat of domestic cattle.

And so Dakotans began the cattle raising that would become an important business on the prairies. The census of 1860 showed only 800 head of cattle on Dakota farms. But ten years later, Dakota Territory had over 56 thousand head of cattle. This number would continue to increase for years to come.

Beef stock did well on the prairie grasses, and fattened satisfactorily. They were able to winter in the open. So thousands more cattle grazed over the prairie land.

From whence did they come? The earliest came from the Middle West, but the largest number were the Longhorn cattle from Texas.

In Texas a Longhorn could be bought for from $3 to $10. Up in Dakota Territory and Montana, it was worth ten times that amount. So Texans drove cattle northward. Some they shipped East by rail at Abilene, Kansas, and others they drove west and north. By the 1870s, Texas cowpunchers were driving their cattle on drives of four to six months into Wyoming, Montana, and Dakota Territory.

A cattle drive from Texas to Dakota was no pleasure trip. Herds of about 2,500 cattle required a trail party of about a dozen men—the boss, a cook, and about a dozen cowboys.

94—Texas "Longhorn" cattle grazing on Dakota prairie

The cook drove his own chuck wagon. Each cowboy had from four to six horses for his own use.

The cook drove ahead, stopping to prepare meals where the stock could get water. Two cowboys rode in advance on opposite sides of the herd to control the cattle at the front. Along the sides of the herd came the flank drivers. In the rear of the herd, the cowboys pushed the stragglers.

A sudden scare could send the herd in wild stampede. Whooping Indians, a wild animal, a sudden flash of lightning or crash of thunder could panic the herd.

At night, cowboys rode guard in three shifts. They sang or whistled as they watched because the cattle seemed more secure with the cowboys moving about them.

Crossing streams often provided trouble. Once the lead cattle had been prodded into swimming across, the rest of the herd would follow. But a sudden noise or strange sight on the opposite shore could excite the cattle into turning back. Cowboys worked desperately to keep frightened cattle swimming across. Sometimes a cowboy would get dumped from his horse while struggling with an obstinate bull. But he usually got back to shore by crawling on the back of a steer or by hanging onto a cow's tail.

Sometimes in a stampede, a rider might be thrown off his horse, then trampled to death under the hundreds of hooves. The other cowboys quickly dug a grave for the mangled body. After covering the grave with rocks to keep animals from digging up the body, the cowboys continued their drive.

Along with the Longhorns were cattle infected with "tick fever." This tick fever could kill cattle, and it infected some buffalo herds. In 1825 in eastern Nebraska an epidemic of such a disease destroyed all the buffaloes there. Another epidemic in 1858 exterminated the buffaloes in the Platte River area.

96—Cattle being driven across a river

97—Cowboys gathered for a roundup

98—Cattle roundup in Badlands country

95—Cowboy camp cook with chuck wagon

IX - Little Bighorn

1 - The Crooked Tongued

When a man could not be trusted to keep his word, the Indian said such a man spoke with a crooked tongue. And more and more the Indians of Dakota declared the white men had crooked tongues.

The Sioux watched as the wagon trains of goldseekers went right through Sioux country where whites had no right to go. And so Sioux warriors captured goldseekers' horses and killings increased. The whites built forts and stationed soldiers to protect goldseekers passing through Indian country.

In April of 1868, about half of the chiefs of the Sioux nation and some chiefs of the Cheyenne tribe met at Fort Laramie with white generals. The whites and redskins signed a treaty of peace. They agreed that this treaty would be kept as long as the streams flowed downward to the great waters. Yes, as long as the grass rippled in the prairie breeze.

For the Sioux nation, the Black Hills was their sacred meeting place. It was part of the Great Sioux Reservation west of the Missouri.

But white trespassers had found traces of gold in the Black Hills. One such trespasser carved a message into a stone on Lookout Mountain some time in the early 1830s: "Got all the gold we could carry. Our ponies were got by the Indians. I have lost my gun and have nothing to eat. Indians are hunting me."

By the 1870s, goldseeking parties refused to stay out of the Black Hills and angry Indians killed many of them. In 1874, General George Custer led an expedition of a thousand men, mostly soldiers, to the Black Hills. They returned with the news that much gold could, indeed, be found in the Black Hills.

Indians followed the ruts cut into the prairie by the yellow-haired general's 110 wagons and they called the ruts "The Trail of the Thieves." From their Cheyenne friends they had learned of Custer's Seventh Cavalry massacre of a hundred Indians in the Washita River valley and their hearts burned with anger against "Yellow Hair."

By the summer of 1875, 800 goldseekers had sneaked into the Black Hills. While soldiers in August drove 600 such miners out, other miners kept sneaking in.

Now the whites tried to get the Sioux to sell their Black Hills, but the chiefs refused to give up their favorite retreat. The U. S. Government took the soldier patrol out of the Black hills, refusing to

99—Freighting supplies to goldseekers in the Black Hills

100—Bismarck Tribune announcement of gold discovered
in the Black Hills

protect any whites who trespassed there. By winter
15,000 goldseekers had swarmed into the Black
Hills. The next spring, they numbered 25,000.

Not only had the crooked-tongued invaded land
that belonged to the Indians, but some of the
provisions of food and clothing intended for Indians
on Reservations reached white men instead. Missouri woodhawks, trappers, and traders obtained
such goods. Some of it even found its way into
Bismarck stores to be sold there.

When James A. Emmons, the publisher of the
Bismarck **Sun**, discovered this corruption, he wrote
about it in his newspaper. The New York **Herald**
also sent out a reporter who uncovered more of the
scandal of how Indians were being cheated.

More and more Sioux warriors agreed with their
chiefs that they must go against these crooked-
tongued whites and drive them out. Sitting Bull, the
medicine man, had visions of many white men
killed.

Fearful that the Sioux would indeed go on the
warpath, the Commissioner of Indian Affairs on
December 6, 1875, ordered that Indian agents
order all Sioux Indians back into Reservations
before January 31, 1876.

Many Indians could not be reached. Some who
heard the Indian agent's order would not take their
women and children out of sheltered camps in the
dead of winter. Other Indians refused to obey the
order—they would fight whites who did not respect
treaties.

The Army generals then decided they would
round up all Indians who refused to return to
Reservations. And Yellow Hair Custer at Fort
Abraham Lincoln—across the Missouri from Bismarck—began building up his command.

101—Custer House, 1876

102—Officers and their wives on the steps of Custer House

Story of the Peace Garden State, page 65

2 - The Greasy Grass

In the Idaho country, General George Crook had defeated the Paiute Indians, and in the Southwest he had whipped the Apaches. Now as word spread that the Sioux were getting ready to drive out the whites, Crook set out with a strong force to teach the Sioux a lesson.

One bitterly cold night in March, 1876, some of his soldiers set fire to the lodges of the village of young Chief Crazy Horse. Indian families escaped, many naked, into the frigid cold. Crazy Horse and his warriors fought like furious hornets, forcing the soldiers back. Then they drove Crook and his frostbitten army back to their Fort Fetterman.

In May, Crook returned to Sioux country, and again Crazy Horse drove the soldiers back. Then while General Crook waited for reinforcements, Crazy Horse and his people hurried to the Little Bighorn encampment where thousands of Sioux and Cheyenne gathered about Sitting Bull. There in the hog-backed hills the Indians called the Greasy Grass, the medicine man told the warriors that his vision of white men killed was surely coming to pass!

The white generals planned that they would come at the hostile Sioux from three directions. General Alfred Terry would lead the command west from Fort Abraham Lincoln. Colonel John Gibbon would bring a Montana force, and General Crook would come north again from Fort Fetterman. Captain Grant Marsh must bring the supply steamer, **Far West**, to the mouth of the Little Bighorn River.

When the Gibbon and Terry commands met near the mouth of Rosebud Creek, they decided only about 1,500 warriors had gathered at the Greasy Grass. Why not attack them without waiting for Crook?

On June 21, General Terry told General George Custer to take his Seventh Cavalry southwestward so Custer could then approach the Indian encampment from the south. Gibbon and Terry would go up the Bighorn and Little Bighorn Rivers and stop the Indians' escape to the north.

The next day, Custer, with 600 soldiers, 44 Indian scouts, and 20 civilian helpers set out. Two nights later his scouts had picked up the Indians' trail. Arikara and Crow scouts reported seeing huge camps of Sioux. But Yellow Hair Custer would not believe the Sioux were in such fearful numbers.

When several Sioux Indians were seen, Custer decided these might be scouts who would warn the encampment to escape. To prevent this, he ordered his troops forward.

Halting briefly, Custer instructed Captain Frederick Benteen to take three companies and scout the bluffs south and west. Then Custer and Major Marcus Reno hurried ahead of the pack train (loaded with ammunition) and marched toward the Little Bighorn.

Early that blistering afternoon, they sighted about forty Sioux warriors. Custer ordered Reno and his 112 weary men and 28 scouts to pursue these warriors. So Reno took leave of his commander, expecting to join him in the attack on the Sioux encampment.

Reno followed the warriors to the Little Bighorn River and crossed it. Then, suddenly, large numbers of Sioux came out to attack. To escape being surrounded, Reno led his men in a wild retreat across the river, up ravines and onto bluff tops.

Exhausted and nearly out of ammunition, with forty of their men missing, the soldiers began digging rifle pits. But the Sioux warriors stopped their fierce attack.

103—General George Armstrong Custer

104—Major Marcus A. Reno

105—Captain Frederick W. Benteen

Then the soldiers heard the sound of distant gunfire to the north. Shortly, Benteen and his men joined the shaken Reno force. The shooting to the north, they decided, must be Custer battling the Sioux. So as soon as the pack train reached them with ammunition, they started northward, carrying their wounded. They must help Custer.

On a high bluff, the first of Reno and Benteen's men could see great numbers of mounted Indians milling about a hill four miles distant. They could see no Seventh Cavalry.

Then they caught sight of a great number of Indians galloping toward them. Benteen and Reno ordered their men back to the high bluffs. Here the soldiers desperately dug rifle pits with butcher knives, tin cups, and a few shovels.

Hiding themselves behind dead and dying horses, the troopers fought back wave after wave of howling warriors until darkness came. Again, the next day, under the hot sun, the Indians kept up their furious attack. From the ravines below, without exposing themselves, they arched arrows to fall upon soldiers in the rifle pits.

With water canteens emptied for hours, wounded men lay almost crazed from thirst. Men volunteered to steal down to the river's edge for water; they did not return.

In late afternoon of June 26, the Indians set fire to the grass along the valley. As the smoke lifted, the soldiers could see a great procession of people and ponies and tepee pole travois trailing west toward the Big Horn Mountains. Only a few warriors fired from ambush, and by evening they disappeared.

Through the night, the soldiers waited. Next day the copper sun seared down on 22 dead and 44 wounded lying upon the bluff tops.

Early in the forenoon, a large dust cloud rose from the sagebrush flat in the valley as Terry and Gibbon's forces advanced toward them. Now Reno and Benteen's men understood why the Indians had gone away.

When General Terry and other men reached the battleground atop the bluffs, "strong men wept on each other's necks." Some of them had already stood in silent horror where Yellow Hair and his 261 men lay dead upon the Greasy Grass.

106—Indian pictograph of the battle at Little Bighorn

107—Reno's retreat site

108—Custer's last stand area

109—Curley, Custer's Crow Indian scout

110—Captain Grant Marsh

3 - Burden Bearer

At the mouth of the Little Bighorn, the **Far West** lay anchored near the willows and cottonwoods of the shore. Suddenly there crashed through the trees a mounted Indian brave. His scalplock stood erect, sign of the Crow tribe. He held his gun high to show that he meant peace.

"It's Curley! Custer's Crow scout!" exclaimed Captain Baker.

Curley urged his jaded horse into the water. When he was pulled on deck, he dropped down beside a chest and sobbed and groaned while the white men stared.

Curley could speak no English. No man aboard the **Far West** could speak Crow.

Captain Baker gave Curley paper and pencil.

The scout drew two circles, one inside the other. Between the circles he covered the space with dots, wailing as he did so, "Sioux! Sioux! Sioux!"

Fewer dots he sprinkled over the inside circle as he cried, "**Absaroka! Absaroka!**"

"**Absaroka!** That's Crow for soldiers," said Captain Marsh.

Curley sprang to his feet and flung his arms wide. Then he beat his breasts. "Poof! Absaroka! Poof! Poof!"

He imitated the Sioux war dance and the taking of scalps. Soldiers had been killed, that much was clear. But how many? Where?

Next dawn, there came the sound of rifle shots, then a single horseman riding wildly away from pursuers. He had spotted the **Far West** in time to save himself. Now he told the **Far West** men that Custer and his men lay dead upon a hill above the Little Bighorn. And four miles further south lay Reno's dead and wounded.

The next morning, two scouts arrived from Terry's command with orders for Captain Marsh. The **Far West** must transport more than fifty wounded men with all speed possible to Fort Lincoln over 700 miles down the treacherous Missouri.

The ship's crew cut tall grass and covered the deck to a depth of 18 inches. Over this they spread tarpaulins to make beds for the wounded.

At two o'clock that night the first of the wounded came on litters made from the hides of dead cavalry horses. By dawn of June 30, 52 suffering men lay upon the great mattress of grass. Soldiers brought aboard, too, the only living survivor found on the Custer battlefield—the badly-wounded horse, Comanche.

Nearly overwhelmed with his responsibility, Captain Marsh swung the **Far West** around and down the Big Horn. Late that afternoon the ship

TRIBUNE EXTRA.

BISMARCK. D. T., JULY 6, 1876.

MASSACRED

EN. CUSTER AND 261 MEN THE VICTIMS.

O OFFICER OR MAN OF 5 COMPANIES LEFT TO

Sioux, emptying several chambers of his revolver, each time bringing a red-skin before he was brought down—shot through the heart. It was here Bloody Knife surrendered his spirit to the one who gave it fighting the natural and hereditary foes of his tribe, as well as the foes of the whites.

The Sioux dashed up beside the soldiers in some instances knocking them from their horses and killing them at their pleasure. This was the case with Lt. McIntosh, who was unarmed except with a saber. He was pulled from his horse, tortured and finally murdered at the pleasure of the red devils. It was here that Fred Girard was separated from the command and lay all night with the

is terribly mutilated. The squaws seem to have passed over the field and crushed the skulls of the wounded and dying with stones and clubs. The heads of some were severed from the body, the privates of some were cut off, while others bore traces of torture, arrows having been shot into their private parts while yet living, or other means of torture adopted. The officers who fell were as follows: Gen. G. A. Custer, Cols. Geo. Yates, Miles Keogh, James Calhoun W. W. Cook, Capts. McIntosh, A. E. Smith, Lieutenants Riley, Critenden, Sturgis, Harrington, Hodgson and Porter. Asst. Surgeon D. Wolf The only citizens killed were Boston Custer, Mr. Reed, Charles Reynolds, Isiah, the interpreter from Ft Rice and Mark Kel-

Gen. Custer, Cols. Calhoun, Yates, Capt Smith, and Lt. Porter. The unhappy Mrs. Calhoun, loses a husband, three brothers and a nephew. Lt. Harrington also had a family, but no trace of his remains was found. We are indebted to Col. Smith for the following full list of the dead; to Dr. Porter for the list of wounded, which is also full:

KILLED.

Field and staff. George A. Custer.
Brevt. Major General.

W. W. Cook, Brevt. Lt-Colonel.
Lord. Asst. Surgeon. J. M. DeWolf,
Acting Asst. Surgeon.

N. C. Staff, W. W. Sharrow, Surg
Major.

Henry Voss, Chief Insptr.

" H. A. Bailey . . . . Black
" J. E. Broadhurst . . . .
" J. Barry . . . .
" J. Conners . . . .
" T. P. Downing . . . .
" Mason . . . .
" Blorm . . . .
" Meyer . . . .
" McElroy . . . .
" Mooney . . . .
" Faker . . . .
" Foyle . . . .
" Bauth . . . .
" Conner . . . .
" Daring . . . .
" Davis . . . .
" Farrell . . . . . .
" Hilcy . . . .
" Huber . . . .
" Hime . . . .

reached the Yellowstone where they must ferry Gibbon's men across the river.

Free on July 2 to go on, the ship sped down the June-flood-swollen river. Sometimes the keel scraped a sandbar, and the boat sheered so violently that soldiers standing guard on deck were thrown like tenpins, and the wounded cried out as they jolted on their grass beds. Around the bends of the river the white boat sped, sometimes driving directly toward the mainland, then miraculously veering in time to avoid hitting the shore.

Nearly 350 miles a day, missing snags and islands and sandbars, the **Far West** raced on. At eleven o'clock the night of July 5, with its flag at halfmast, it reached Bismarck.

Men ran from the ship to awaken the sleeping town with the news of a tragedy that would stun all America. Down at Fort Abraham Lincoln 28 widows wept in a nightmare of sorrow.

camps at $1. And out beyond the Greasy Grass, Sitting Bull boasted that he had made great medicine that had brought death to Yellow Hair and the crooked-tongued ones.

The killing of 261 white men stung the nation. All the rights to hunting grounds were now taken from the Sioux. And white farmers, cattlemen, and prospectors looked with eager eye upon the vast lands that once belonged to the Sioux.

While military men pursued them, the Sioux split into small bands, some escaping across the border into Canada, almost without food and clothing. Others returned to Reservations in the United States.

Bitter winters in the northern plains brought hunger and freezing cold. At last the proud conquerors of Yellow Hair straggled back, beaten in spirit, and gaunt of body. Back they came to Reservations to beg food and shelter from the Great White Father's hand.

4 - Tribune Extra

At Bismarck, C. A. Lounsberry, editor of the Bismarck **Tribune**, hurried to the telegraph office. He brought with him General Terry's official list of the dead and the wounded. He had notes written by Mark Kellogg, a brilliant newspaper reporter who had died with Custer. The Indians had left the notes undisturbed in the pouch of the "man who makes the paper talk." Officers from the **Far West** had told Lounsberry what they knew.

So the editor pieced together a 50,000-word press release to be sent over the wires to the New York **Herald**. At the same time, he furnished copy for his own **Tribune** typesetters.

The New York **Herald** ran a 14-column story about the Custer Massacre. The first published report in the **Tribune** sold on the streets of Bismarck for 25 cents a copy and in Montana mining

112—The Helena transporting Sioux Indians back to Standing Rock Reservation

X - Dakota Boom

1 - The Empire Builder

In Saint Paul, Minnesota, young Jim Hill watched the Red River Carts come and go. For a time he worked as a clerk for steamers on the Mississippi; there he saw train equipment arriving on Mississippi barges. One day in June, 1862, he thrilled to the chuff-chuffing of the first locomotive in Minnesota as it pulled two passenger cars from Saint Paul to the village of St. Anthony (Minneapolis).

The shipping business more and more captured Jim Hill's interest. In 1871 he invested in a steamship partnership on the Red River and became enthusiastic about the farming possibilities in the Red River Valley. He soon owned his own Red River Transportation Company and became a wealthy man.

When the St. Paul Pacific Railway bankrupted, Jim Hill, Norman Kittson, and two Canadian friends bought the railway company. He and his partners kept buying several small railways in Minnesota and building more track.

Jim Hill decided how he would continue to build his own railway. He wanted his rail lines to bring in homesteaders who would farm. Farmers would grow crops for his railway to ship to market. Out from his main railway he built short feeder lines where farmers could drive their wagons to shipping points.

Homesteaders settled all about Hill's railway lines. Because the settlers prospered, so did Hill's railway company. He added more rail lines as he could afford it, for he did not believe in borrowing money.

On March 10, 1880, his first train rumbled over the newly-built bridge at Grand Forks, the only celebration being the peppy whistling of the locomotive. That summer Hill's railway fanned into the Dakota side of the Red River Valley, its feeder lines spreading out to encourage settlers to come and farm. On July 4, three years later, the railroad reached Devils Lake. By 1886 it built to the tent town of Minot and on to Gasman Coulee four miles west.

113—Jim Hill

At that time, Fort Berthold Indian Reservation extended north and west from the Missouri River. The U. S. Government served notice that Hill could not build his railway into Indian territory.

Congress a year later allowed Hill to buy railway right-of-way from the Fort Berthold Indians. During that year of waiting for permission to build further, Hill's company stockpiled construction materials at Minot. Stacks of ties, timbers, piling, sawed lumber, kegs of spikes and bolts covered acres of ground. The railway cars that unloaded this construction material did not return empty to Eastern markets but transported there the bleached bones of Uncle Buffalo.

Hill declared that the track must reach Great Falls, Montana, before winter set in. For this reason, 8,000 men gathered in Minot that spring of 1887 to work on the grading westward. About one-fourth of these men operated the one-man scrapers drawn by mules or horses. Over 3,300 horses and mules pulled the scrapers. An additional 225 teams worked with 650 men who laid ties and track. Except for the work locomotive which followed up the track laying, men and horses did all the work.

By 1890 the railway companies in which Jim Hill had major ownership took the name of Great Northern Railway Company and three years later completed its route to the Pacific.

By this time, branchlines from the Great Northern, the Northern Pacific, and two other lines (Soo & Chicago, and Milwaukee-St.Paul) had brought the rail mileage in North Dakota to 2,507.

Up until the building of the railroads, transportation had been only north and south—along the Red and Missouri Rivers. The railways brought transportation east and west, and eventually ended the riverboat commerce.

Jim Hill's railway business made him a multimillionaire. He became known as the "Empire Builder" because his interest and efforts brought thousands of settlers into the country. Even to the end of his life, he traveled about, speaking to farmers and helping them to use better methods. He hired agricultural experts to lecture and to demonstrate to farmers. He bought purebred livestock and gave these to farmers. In one year alone, he gave away fifty Shorthorn bulls costing about $500 each.

114—Great Northern track laying

115—Group of Dunkard settlers

2 - Immigrant Homesteaders

When Jim Hill's railway began stretching out over Dakota Territory, the Northern Pacific had reached nearly across the territory to Montana.

Free prairie land waited for homesteaders. Farm land lay ready for the breaking plow, free of stumps, trees, and underbrush. The stony hills along the Missouri offered good grazing for cattle. The labor-saving machinery demonstrated on the bonanza farms could be put to good use on a homesteader's farm.

With all of Minnesota and Iowa settled, newspapers and people in those states no longer told stories about people in Dakota Territory freezing to death in terrible blizzards. And as news spread about the great coal deposits in western Dakota, Easterners quit telling tales of how Dakota homesteaders had to burn twisted hay. corn cobs, and buffalo chips as they huddled about their shanty stoves.

116—Early train in east central North Dakota

Story of the Peace Garden State, page 71

117—Interior of immigrant car (Harper's Weekly, February 10, 1883)

120—Homesteader and wife bringing a cart of buffalo bones to market

118—Immigrant car leaving Saint Paul Union station (Harper's Weekly, September 13, 1886)

121—Piles of buffalo bones awaiting shipment at rail station

119—Landseekers from Iowa, 1898

122—Oxen pulling an early grain binder (F. Jay Haynes photo)

The 1870 census showed about 2,000 people living in the northern part of Dakota Territory. But ten years later, this population had multiplied by 18.

Dakota Territory set up an immigration office and sent out pamphlets and posters advertising the free and fertile land in Dakota. Many of these pamphlets were printed in the languages of northern European countries where peasants struggled to make a living on tiny patches of land. Or they worked in cities and lived in poverty. To such people, Dakota Territory sounded like the Land of Promise, a wonderland where just by living on it a man and his family could get 160 acres of land!

A hundred years earlier, the Russian czar had encouraged Germans to settle in southern Russia. Now in 1871 the Russian Government made the Germans subject to military draft. The Germans were also told that in ten years they must learn to use the Russian language and they must adopt the Russian Orthodox religion—or get out of Russia. A hundred thousand of these German-Russians then emigrated and reached America in three years, many of them finding their way to Dakota.

Railway companies sent men to the British Isles and to Norway, Sweden, Denmark, Holland, Switzerland, and Germany to encourage people to emigrate to Dakota. Advertisements of Dakota land appeared in American, Canadian, and northern European newspapers.

And so during the first "Great Dakota Boom," the population of North Dakota increased more than a thousand percent.

Land seekers poured into Dakota both from Europe and from the states to the east. They came in colonies which settled entire communities, but most of these home builders came as single persons or with their families.

By 1885, people in the northern part of Dakota Territory numbered over 152,000. When the northern part of Dakota Territory became the state of North Dakota, half of the Territory had been homesteaded. In the northwestern part of North Dakota, homesteading would continue until 1912.

Most of the people who settled North Dakota did not come in ox-drawn covered wagons but by train. Immigrants could not afford fare on regular passenger coaches, so railway companies built simple immigrant cars for them. Such immigrant cars boasted no fancy decorations or soft cushions. Passengers slept on plank bunks, and they brought their own food.

American farmers, seeking a new start in the West, loaded their livestock and belongings into freight cars. The farmer would ride with his livestock while his family rode in an immigrant car or passenger coach. It was not unusual for a father to smuggle teenage sons with him in the freight car.

The Great American Desert had become for thousands of people truly the Land of Promise.

3 - Colony Settlements

After hunger, bitter cold, and the pestilence of smallpox a third of Icelanders had died at their Gimli colony near Lake Winnipeg in Canada. To them came the young Reverend Pall Thorlackson, urging them to find better living in the United States.

He had come from Wisconsin, hoping to bring this suffering colony of Icelanders there. But aboard a Red River steamer, the captain had told him about the fertile Red River Valley where land and timber waited free.

Weakened by suffering, and fearful they would find life no better away from Gimli, the Icelanders would not leave. Only a few young men listened and

123—Tar-papered shanty insulated with sod

124—Log cabin near Velva, 1886

125—Colony arrives to settle Hettinger

126—Colony moving to North Dakota under guidance of Max Bass, Great Northern Railway immigration agent

followed the pastor to Winnipeg where he found jobs for them.

Meanwhile, two young Icelanders decided to seek out the promised land in the United States and walked to Pembina. They found land they liked along the Tongue River. Here Pastor Thorlackson and two other young men discovered them, and together they happily built their first cabin.

Thorlackson returned to Gimli to bring more settlers. But not until after another winter of suffering did he succeed in bringing the first band of settlers back with him to the Tongue River area. Thus began the Icelandic communities in what is now northeastern North Dakota.

Other colonies came by train. Fifty families were the first of Russian farmers to settle west of the Missouri. Seventy-five Hollander families located in what is now Emmons County. A Methodist colony from Wisconsin found homes in the Sterling vicinity east of Bismarck. A Polish community settled at Crystal Springs. West of the Missouri, along the Northern Pacific, such towns as New Salem, Glen Ullin, Richardton, Taylor, Gladstone, Dickinson,

and Belfield were mostly started by large groups of settlers.

A German immigrant, Max Bass, served as immigration agent for the Great Northern Railway. He brought a colony of 350 German Baptist Brethren to settle the Cando area. The special train consisted of 38 freight cars and nine passenger cars. Large banners on the car proclaimed: "From Indiana to the Rich, Free Government Lands in North Dakota, via the famous Red River Valley, the Bread Basket of the World."

In Norway, a government official by the name of Paul Hjelm-Hansen, decided that Norwegian laborers and tenant farmers would be wise to move to America where they could get free land. In 1867, he came to America himself and got a job writing for a Norwegian newspaper at LaCrosse, Wisconsin.

Later, he got himself an ox-cart and went exploring the Red River Valley. He liked what he saw. He prophesied that within ten years the Red River Valley would become one of the greatest farming regions in America. All that was needed, he said, was for Norwegian immigrants to come there and cultivate the wilderness. His writings were published in Norwegian papers in the United States as well as newspapers in Norway.

Thousands of Norwegians migrated, many of them settling in the Red River Valley. Others got on the Great Northern Railway and stopped off on feeder lines along the way. And this accounts for the fact that from the Red River Valley and west over the northern part of North Dakota you will today find that most people are of Norwegian descent.

By 1910 when most of the homesteading by immigrants had been completed, we find that Norwegians accounted for 21 per cent of the population. The Germans and German-Russians who settled the south central part of the state accounted for 20 per cent of North Dakota people. English, including Canadians, supplied 12 percent of the population, Swedes 5 percent. The rest of the foreign-born settlers came from Armenia, Belgium, Bohemia, Bulgaria, Denmark, Finland, France, Greece, Holland, Iceland, Poland and Russia. The largest segment of homesteaders (29 percent) were American- born.

4 - "Wrong Side Up"

A young German immigrant, John Christiansen, joined a company of German immigrants to settle in western Dakota Territory. The colonists, their families and all personal belongings crowded into half a dozen immigrant cars.

John, the youngest of the colonists, rode in a freight car with his team of horses, his wagon, hay and oats, food for himself, and some property belonging to three friends. When the freight train stopped at Jamestown, John bought a breaking plow and tied it to the top of his box car.

John's freight train continued a day ahead of the immigrant cars. His train came to a stop where the town of New Salem was to be built. On planks laid across a ditch, John led his horses out of the box car. The train then moved a short distance ahead and dumped everything out of John's car.

He led his horses to the scattered belongings and tried in vain to find his tent. Snow still lay in large drifts that April 4, 1883. A chill wind blew as John sought shelter in a huddle of boxes. Night fell and shortly the howling of coyotes filled the air. John thought of the ferocious wolves of Europe and shuddered. He dared not fall asleep.

At dawn the immigrant train arrived, stopped long enough for John's three friends to get off. Then it steamed ahead several miles to a siding, leaving the immigrant cars there while train crew men built the New Salem siding.

The colonists were then brought back to the New Salem siding. They lived in the immigrant cars while they built a three-room dwelling, 30 by 40 feet. Into this building everybody then moved, and soon discovered that other colonists had come with them to the prairie. Bedbugs from Minnesota lumber camps had stowed away on the pine boards and timbers.

During that first summer, the colonists scattered about on homesteads. Each family built a small frame shanty—from which the industrious wives soon exterminated the bedbugs.

No spring or flowing stream could be found in the vicinity. So with spades the men dug a well 8 feet across and 40 feet deep. From this they gained a good supply of water.

Meanwhile, John got busy with his breaking plow, turning an acre of sod on each of about fifteen homestead claims. His was the only plow in the colony and so he earned $5 an acre for his work.

While he was breaking sod on his own homestead, a caravan of two Indian families stopped by. John had never seen an Indian before. He was surprised when one Indian greeted him with, "How, John!" He did not then know that **John** was a usual name an Indian used when he spoke to a white man.

Slowly then, the Indian man stooped and began turning the plowed sod back into its furrow. He patted it carefully into place as he kept saying something over and over again in his own Sioux language.

An Indian boy of about fifteen years joined the group and he translated for John, "He say, 'Wrong side up, wrong side up.'" Soon after, the Indians continued on their way, leaving John Christiansen to ponder what the Indian meant.

The New Salem settlers planted grain upon the acres of prairie turned wrong side up. Seven years

127—Monument erected on the spot where the Sioux Indian advised John Christiansen he was turning the sod wrong side up

of poor crops followed. Some settlers left in discouragement.

John remembered the Indian's words, "Wrong side up, wrong side up." Surely that Indian knew nothing about white man's farming, but he had lived in this prairie land. He must know the land better than immigrant homesteaders.

John and the people of New Salem looked upon the grassy hills where the ground still lay right side up, and they brought milk cows to graze there instead of turning more sod wrong side up. And a new prosperity followed which made New Salem one of the leading dairy centers of North Dakota.

Today "Salem Sue," the largest cow in the world, stands 38 feet high and 50 feet long on a hill between Interstate 94 and the city of New Salem. This fiberglass Holstein calls attention to the dairy industry of the area and lures hundreds of tourists each summer to walk about under her and enjoy a spectacular view of the surrounding countryside.

128—"Salem Sue," the world's largest Holstein cow, calls attention to the New Salem dairy industry

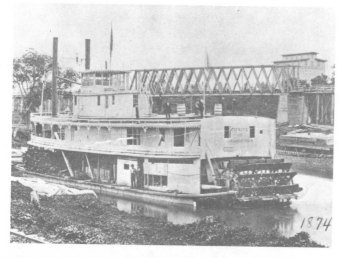

129—The Selkirker, the "Floating Palace of the Red River"

132—Missouri River steamer, Rosebud

130—The Minnie-H on Devils Lake

131—Newspaper advertisement of the Nellie Baldwin launched on the James River

133—The U. S. S. Mandan, snag boat used for clearing the Missouri channel of snags and sawyers during the late years of river traffic

5 - Steamboat Exit

On the Red River, the railway gave new life to boat traffic. The interior of Canada opened for settlement, so the Red River provided a good route for immigrants going there. The Red River Carts gave way to the safer transportation that Jim Hill's steamer, **The Selkirker**, could provide.

For nearly ten years after the Northern Pacific railroad reached Fargo, fifteen different steamers traveled the Red River, and did good business. Some Red River boats towed up to 12 barges behind them. Hundreds of such barges were built at Fargo and other river points, loaded heavily and floated downstream, guided by men steering at tillers. When they arrived at their destination and unloaded. the flatboats were then taken apart and the lumber used for building houses, most of these in the Winnipeg area.

As settlement increased in the Red River Valley and into Canada, steamers and barges carried great loads of lumber, livestock, threshing machines, farm machinery and general supplies. Passengers found little space to walk on the decks. Persons who could not afford cabins slept on stacks of freight.

Rails and a locomotive for the Canadian Pacific Railway, an entire circus bound for Winnipeg, kegs of liquor—the steamers carried whatever business brought them. They brought to Fargo grain from farmers and the slowly diminishing furs and hides from lands yet unsettled.

Then the railway which had brought new river business gradually brought an end to it as rails reached points along the Red River. By 1877 commercial steamboating on the Red was about finished. No longer would steamboats swing round the bends of the crookedest river in the world.

At Devils Lake, Captain Edward Heerman launched his **Minnie-H** on July 4, 1883. For sixteen years it carried passengers and freight between Devils Lake, Fort Totten, and Minnewaukan.

In 1880, Anton Klaus, a Jamestown merchant, built a sternwheeler 75 feet long and 14 feet wide and slid it into the James River. It had one season in that shallow stream and then was hauled to Spiritwood Lake to be used as an excursion boat. The encyclopedia proved right when it declared: "The James River is the longest unnavigable river in the world."

For more than ten years after the Northern Pacific reached Bismarck, Missouri river steamers enjoyed good business. Between 30 and 40 boats sailed from Bismarck to serve towns along the upper Missouri and the Yellowstone. But when Hill's Great Northern puffed into Helena, Montana, in 1877, river traffic became limited to steamers shipping from points between Williston and Bismarck. Captain Grant Marsh retired to Washburn, operating grain and lumber boats from there until his death in 1916.

Gasoline engines took the place of steam power on the few remaining boats. The U. S. Government quit operating its snag boats, and in 1936 the Benton Packet Company quit operating its last boat on the Big Muddy.

Like Uncle Buffalo, the colorful river steamer disappeared from Dakota.

6 - Beef Bonanza

After the Sioux and Cheyenne defeated Custer on the hills of Greasy Grass, an angry Congress reduced the sizes of Indian Reservations. With the buffalo almost exterminated, great stretches of prairie grass could provide forage for cattle. So began the brief years of the open-range rancher.

Such a man simply found himself a "spread" of land where no other white man lived, and he claimed it as his range. He would own the quarter section of land on which he placed his buildings, but he had no legal right to the lands he claimed for his livestock. He built no fences. So his cattle wandered freely about, often mixing with stock from neighboring spreads.

As wealthy Easterners had done for early bonanza wheat farms, they now decided to get richer by financing the cattle and equipment on Dakota spreads. Most such financiers could not tell a branding iron from a stove poker.

Ranchers in Texas brought about three-fourths of the open-range stock into what is now western North Dakota. Between 1866 and 1885 Texans trailed nearly six million cattle to the northern ranges. Several ranches were thus established, chiefly in the Little Missouri and Badlands country, though there were several ranches also in the Souris River area.

Cattle were also driven into North Dakota ranges from Colorado, Washington, Oregon, Wisconsin, Minnesota, Michigan, Illinois and Iowa. Cattle brought from such states were generally known as "Pilgrims"; those brought up from Texas were "Longhorns."

The Longhorn could take care of itself during warm weather, but it lacked hardihood for cold winters. It had long slender legs, a bony frame, and a big head with sharp horns four to five feet from tip to tip. It did not bring as good a price at Eastern markets as did the heavier farm Pilgrim from corn belt states.

134—Cover of book telling how to make good money in the cattle business

On the open ranges, cattle thieves known as "rustlers" stole freely, and cleverly re-branded their stolen stock. Wolves and coyotes killed young cattle. Indians from Reservations also helped themselves to the white man's buffalo.

In ranch country where people lived many miles apart, there was no law officer. So ranchers organized cattlemen's associations which regulated cattle brands and breeding. They also organized or supported "Vigilante" groups of men who took the law into their own hands and hunted down rustlers and often hanged them.

The cattlemen's associations also organized the spring roundup. On the open range, some cattle from neighboring ranches might get mixed together. So on the spring roundup, cowboys from each ranch would identify their owner's cows by their brands, rope their young calves and brand them. Then in the fall when cattle were ready for market, a second roundup selected cattle to drive off to the nearest railway shipping point. They also would brand any calves they might have missed during the spring roundup.

A succession of open winters with little snow brought good profits for the cattlemen. This resulted in more and more cattle being brought in until by the summer of 1886 the ranges were badly overstocked. Hot winds shriveled the grass. Beaver dams broke down because beavers had been trapped almost to extinction. So where the buffalo of olden times had found water, the range cattle now found only dry creek beds. Since beef prices kept dropping, ranchers did not want to sell. Some Montana

135—Cowboys in front of the HT Ranch horse barn

and Wyoming ranchers drove their cattle north into Canada to find grass for them.

While the range cattle grew scrawny on the sparse thin grass that autumn, Dakota oldtimers observed that the few beavers who remained stored extra large numbers of saplings for their winter food supply. The oldtimers said the bark on the cottonwood trees had grown thicker than usual. The blackbirds flocked much earlier, and the Arctic owl returned sooner than usual. Great platoons of ducks and geese winged southward six weeks ahead of time.

7 - The Great White Ruin

By early November, 1886, blizzards swirled over the prairies, and the scrawny cattle headed into coulees and ravines for shelter. Storm after storm followed, covering the prairies with four to five feet of snow. Huge drifts built leeward of winds. A thaw in January followed by extreme cold put a hard crust on the snow.

Open-range cattlemen did not store hay to feed their cattle in winter. In the open winters, most of the cattle had hustled for their own forage and few had died. But now as the Texas Longhorns and the Pilgrims from corn belt farms huddled into coulees and ravines, they died from the intense cold, from snow that smothered them, and from starvation. The thick-furred wolves and coyotes closed in for easy kills.

It is believed that over the western plains of America that winter of "The Great White Ruin," more than 300 people lost their lives. Cattlemen died trying to rescue their stock. Even women and children on homesteads, in the distance between the barn and house, lost their way in a blinding blizzard, and some died only a few yards from their own door.

Warm Chinook winds came in early March and melted snows into carcass-filled creek beds. Within days, flooded creeks carried hundreds upon hundreds of the frozen bodies of cattle into the Little Missouri River and on into the Big Muddy.

The snow melted and the carcasses thawed and the stench of rotting flesh filled the April air. Only here and there did some bony animal totter about. Many of these had to be killed because of frozen legs or tails.

The loss of cattle on ranches ran from 50 to as high as 95 percent. Some cattlemen quit the country without trying to round up the remnants of their livestock. Most of the large cattle companies bankrupted. Wealthy Eastern and European men would invest no more money on the Dakota open range.

Only a few large outfits grazed dwindled herds until homesteaders in the early 1900s pushed them off their open ranges. The small rancher and the farmer who could provide their herds with winter shelter and hay took the place of the bonanza cattle companies.

Again the bone gatherers gleaned the prairies and men remembered, for years after, the grim lesson of what the Sioux called the Plenty Snow Winter.

8 - Badlands Dude

Several wealthy Europeans and men of noble blood came to Dakota to hunt and to establish ranches. The most notable of these arrived in Little Missouri, "the toughest town on the Northern Pacific," in April, 1883. He came in a private railway car, for he was very rich and he belonged to the French royal family.

He was Antoine Amedee Marie Vincent Manca de Vallombrosa, the Marquis de Mores, and he had recently married the beautiful daughter of a wealthy New York banker. Cowpokes at the Little Missouri station made fun of this expensively-dressed gentleman with the upturned waxed mustache, and they called him a "dude."

This Marquis de Mores had not come just to enter the ranching business; he wanted also to build a meatpacking plant where cattle were raised. This would cut the cost of transporting. There would be no shrinking of weight in transit. Consumers would pay much less for their meat!

136—The Marquis de Mores

Story of the Peace Garden State, page 79

137—Chateau de Mores

138—The de Mores packing plant at Medora

139—The de Mores Medora-Deadwood stage coach

So he built a meatpacking plant, three ice houses and other buildings for slaughtering cattle. And because he did not care for the rowdy little town of Little Missouri, he built his own little town and named it Medora after his wife.

On a hillside nearby, he built a 26-room summer chateau and staffed it with 20 servants. He and his wife were both excellent marksmen and they went hunting, traveling about in an elegant coach.

But the meatpacking did not bring profit and so after three years, the Marquis put a sign on the costly plant which read: "Rent free to any responsible party who will make use of it." (Forty years later, at Fargo and Grand Forks, meatpacking plants operated profitably. By 1990, there were 20 meatpacking plants in the state.)

The packing plant, however, was just one of the Marquis' businesses. He also shipped salmon from Portland, Oregon, to New York at a profit. He dreamed of a pottery plant in the Badlands and of a great dairy farm there. He established a stage-coach and freighting service between Medora and Deadwood in the Black Hills; but after a few years this failed.

No one knows how much money the Marquis lost in his Badlands businesses, but we do know that he paid every man in full who had helped him or invested in his business.

Today all that remains of the packing plant is its towering smokestack, for the buildings burned down in 1907. The Marquis' little town of Medora outlived the town of Little Missouri, and several of the buildings he built still stand.

When the de Mores family left Medora, they took from their elegant chateau only their servants. The completely-furnished house was left in the care of J. W. Foley, the father of North Dakota's poet laureate. In 1936 the eldest son of the Marquis donated the chateau and the nearby grounds to the State Historical Society of North Dakota, and it is now preserved as the De Mores Historic Site. Thousands of people each year tour the chateau to see the century-old furnishings, the huge fireplace opening into four rooms, the be-ruffled clothes once worn by three little De Mores children, and the private offices of the Marquis and of the Marquise.

9 - Old Four Eyes

Some months after the Marquis de Mores had come to the Badlands, a bespectacled young man of 25 arrived from New York. He wanted to hunt buffalo, so he hired Joe Ferris as a guide.

Joe took this Easterner out in a buckboard and found an old buffalo bull. When he was able to shoot the buffalo down, the young man was so happy he gave Joe a hundred dollar bill on the spot.

A member of the New York state legislature, young Teddy Roosevelt had money and a Harvard education. As a child he had been sickly, weak, and near-sighted. But he wanted to get strong and so had learned to ride horses and to box. As he grew stronger, he became a very good boxer.

He found the Dakota climate and the Badlands country to his liking. So before he returned to New York, he invested $14,000 in a Maltese Cross Ranch partnership.

The following winter both his wife and mother died on the same day. Heavy-hearted, he returned to the Badlands the next summer. Here he found comfort in the beauty of the Badlands and would often ride about, sometimes with a book in his saddlebag so that he could read in the quiet of the outdoors.

Though he tried, he never became much of a cowboy. He gave much of his time to writing books and hunting, and because of his spectacles, the cowboys called him "Four Eyes."

Since his ranch prospered, he invested in another spread, the Elkhorn, and lived in the Badlands for three years. During that time he organized the Little Missouri Stockmen's Association.

One bitterly cold day, he trailed some stray horses and stopped at tiny Mingusville to rest and warm himself. The only heated place was a saloon. While Roosevelt spread his hands before the stove, a drunkard yelled at him, "Four Eyes is going to set up drinks for us!"

Roosevelt tried to ignore the man, but the drunkard, wearing two pistols, would not leave him alone. So Roosevelt stood up, walloped the man on the jaw. With both guns blasting wildly, the gunman dropped to the floor and gave no more trouble.

From that time on, the cowboys always called Roosevelt **Old** Four Eyes.

In April, 1886, when the ice had gone out of the Little Missouri, Old Four Eyes found his boat stolen just when he needed it. So his Elkhorn Ranch partners, William Sewall and Wilmot Dow, built a crude boat and the three of them started down the river to find the thieves. On the third day, they discovered the thieves' camp and shortly captured three men.

After taking their shoes from the thieves, Roose-

140—Teddy Roosevelt, rancher

velt and his partners took the three men down to the Killdeer Mountains vicinity. Here Roosevelt left the thieves under Sewall and Dow's guard while he found a settler who had a wagon and a team of horses.

Roosevelt hired the settler to help him transport the thieves to Dickinson while Sewall and Dow took the boat back to the Elkhorn Ranch.

The weather was too cold to tie the prisoners' hands and feet. So for 36 hours Old Four Eyes dared not sleep. He walked behind the wagon so he could better watch the thieves in the wagon. When he finally delivered the three to the Dickinson jail, he decided to find a doctor to help him with his sore and aching feet.

141—The Roosevelt cabin

Dr. Hugo Stickney later reported to his wife: "I've just met the most peculiar, and at the same time, the most wonderful man I've ever come to know."

The winter of "The Great White Ruin," Roosevelt was in London and there married Edith Carow, a childhood friend. After losing most of his livestock that winter, Roosevelt gradually gave up ranching in Dakota and went back only to visit.

He returned to politics and became President of the United States (1901-1909). He always said, "I would never have been President if it had not been for my experiences in North Dakota."

The Elkhorn Ranch where Old Four Eyes gained more spiritual and physical strength is now part of the Theodore Roosevelt National Memorial Park. His Maltese Cross cabin, after being exhibited at expositions in the United States, and several years on the capitol grounds at Bismarck, is now back in the Badlands near Medora.

10 - A New Capital

In the early years of Dakota Territory, Dakota Assemblymen from the northern Pembina district were called the "Custom House Gang." They represented fur traders, trappers, hunters and the Metis.

Few frontiersmen remained in the southeastern part of Dakota. To Yankton, the capital city, there came lawyers, merchants, land speculators, newspaper editors, and outsiders trying to make a fast buck and then leave. The residents who wanted to make permanent homes in the area were Scandinavian homesteaders. Good crops and the raising of more and more cattle brought increasing prosperity to farmers. Southern Dakota boasted a population of over 60,000—the number of people needed in order for a territory to become a state.

The Gold Rush in the Black Hills brought swarms of people there. It also brought prosperity to southeastern Dakota Territory. Sioux Falls flour mills supplied flour to Deadwood and other mining towns. Yankton merchants shipped large quantities of supplies into the Hills, and they outfitted hundreds of goldseekers. There were so many white people in the Hills that they talked of making their area a separate Territory of Lincoln.

But when the Custom House Gang must attend the Assembly, they had to go to Saint Paul, Minnesota, in order to reach the capital of Dakota Territory.

Newspapers had long urged that the capital be moved to a more central location. Northern Dakotans were especially indignant over the extreme southern location at Yankton. As one Grand Forks editor wrote, a man could go to New York City from northern Dakota almost as quickly as he could reach Yankton by way of Saint Paul.

During the 1883 session of the Assembly, a capital removal bill was pushed through. It provided for a nine-man commission with power to select a new capital site. It further provided that any city interested in becoming the capital of Dakota Territory could bid for the honor by supplying $100,000 and 160 acres of land on which to build the capitol.

The people of Yankton were furious and did all they could to oppose the removal. But the nine men of the Commission visited each of the towns which had bid. In southern Dakota there were six: Aberdeen, Huron, Mitchell, Ordway, Pierre, and Redfield. Three northern Dakota towns bid: Bismarck, Odessa, and Steele. (Ordway, a short distance northeast of Aberdeen, and Odessa on the east end of Devils Lake have long since been forgotten, for they existed only on paper.)

On June 1, the Commission men met at Fargo to

142—Sitting Bull, carrying the U. S. flag, leads the parade to the capitol cornerstone laying, Bismarck, 1883

cast their ballots. After voting thirteen times, they selected Bismarck.

Real estate boomed in Bismarck as plans were made for building the capitol there. Town lots that had been worth $200 to $300 sold for $1,000 or more. The two-thousand residents of Bismarck dug into their pockets to raise the $200,000 and the Northern Pacific Railway donated 160 acres north of the city.

Capitol cornerstone laying ceremonies took place on September 5, 1883. Sitting Bull, carrying the American flag, led the parade to the capitol grounds. Following in that parade were U. S. senators, state governors, city mayors, Henry Villard (president of the Northern Pacific Railway), Secretary of the Interior Henry M. Teller, and General U. S. Grant.

One young woman did her best to impress the distinguished visitors with the new capital city. She tied three bushels of apples to a young tree in her yard. When General Grant was shown this evidence of northern Dakota's fruitfulness, he exclaimed: "Magnificent! I am surprised, wonderfully surprised!"

143—Territorial capitol at Bismarck

11 - Struggle for Statehood

After the capital was moved to Bismarck, southern Dakotans more and more wanted a state of their own. A convention of southern Dakota residents met at Sioux Falls during the harvest season of 1883 and wrote a constitution for their "State of Dakota." But Congress was not impressed.

In northern Dakota, people feared that if southern Dakota became a state, then northern Dakota would continue as a territory much longer. They also wanted to keep the Bismarck capital for the entire area. When the Dakota Assembly met for its first term at Bismarck, it passed a bill relocating the capital at Pierre. But Governor Gilbert A. Pierce vetoed the bill and so kept the seat of government at Bismarck.

For several years, southern Dakotans held conventions in efforts to persuade Congress to grant them statehood. They elected state officers that would be ready to govern as soon as statehood was granted.

As in the earlier years of Dakota Territory, there was much cheating and fraud practiced by appointed territorial officers. And there was Alex McKenzie, a political boss who managed much control behind the scenes. But his fraud and underhanded control was finally discovered and he was sentenced to a Federal prison.

Finally, when the total population of Dakota Territory had reached half a million, voting showed a small majority as favoring the division of Dakota Territory into a southern state and a northern

territory. Delegate O. S. Gifford presented bills in Congress which, for the first time, asked for the admission of two states, North Dakota, and South Dakota.

In the closing session of Congress, 1889, the Omnibus Bill was passed, making it possible for Montana, North Dakota, South Dakota, and Washington to be admitted as states as soon as state constitutions were approved and state officials elected.

President Cleveland signed this act on Washington's birthday, using a pen made from the quill of a Dakota eagle.

The Omnibus Bill provided that people in the North Dakota area should elect 75 men to hold a state convention at Bismarck, opening July 4. The people would vote on the constitution in October.

The bill provided that the lands set aside for Indian Reservations and military forts should continue to be United States Government property. All Territory debts must be divided between the states.

General William Henry Harrison Beadle was the territorial superintendent of public instruction. He had long tried to make sure schools would have money for building and operation. His plan to help schools was adopted: two sections of land in each township in a state would be set aside as school land. These could not be sold for less than ten dollars an acre. Beadle's plan was made law in the Omnibus Bill. Also in North Dakota, 500,000 acres were set aside for the support of state institutions.

12 - Red Messiah

After the Custer Massacre, most white people felt little kindness toward the Sioux Indians. U. S. Army expeditions relentlessly hunted down any Sioux not on a Reservation. Chief Crazy Horse and other Sioux leaders surrendered. Sitting Bull and his band escaped into Canada. While no white soldiers followed him there, he found Canadian whites unwilling to help him, and his enemies became the cold and the hunger.

On the Reservation, the Indian warrior had to give up his gun. He was not allowed to take part in the Sun Dance. His children were sent to school and taught to live like whites. They must turn their backs on the red man's heritage.

Railroads brought thousands of settlers who turned the sod of hunting grounds wrong side up. Ranchers drove in their thousands of cattle where once Uncle Buffalo had roamed. When Agency rations were not enough to satisfy his hunger, many an Indian made a bow and arrows and killed a white man's steer in a hidden ravine. Had the white man been hungry when he slaughtered Uncle Buffalo?

Whipped at last by hunger, Sitting Bull led his people back from Canada in July, 1881, and surrendered at Fort Buford. He was put in prison for two years at Fort Randall, then allowed to live on Standing Rock Indian Reservation.

In 1885 he toured America with Buffalo Bill Cody's Wild West Show. Here he earned an extra income by charging $1.50 for his autograph—which a Canadian priest had taught him to write.

Then a new sort of religion came from a Paiute Indian who had once lived in a white man's home. This came about on January 1, 1889, when the sun eclipsed. While his people trembled in fear that the

145—Sitting Bull with Buffalo Bill Cody on tour

sun had died, this Wovoka claimed he had a vision that the Great Spirit had chosen him to lead his people. Wovoka claimed himself to be a second Messiah, this time in Indian flesh.

According to Wovoka's teachings, a new age would come to the Indian if he would faithfully perform the Ghost Dance as the Great Spirit had instructed Wovoka.

The Sioux Indians heard of this Red Messiah that would come from the West. Before him would come a great earth-wave to bury the whites forever under. Uncle Buffalo would come riding a-top this great earth-wave so again there would be plenty for the Indian. Indeed, the Indian dead would come back from the Green Grass World to inherit the wonderful new hunting grounds with the living Indians.

144—Ghost dancers at Standing Rock Reservation

How would the Indian escape being buried with the white man under the great earth-wave? He must faithfully join in the Ghost Dance for four successive nights every six weeks. Then when the new earth came rolling over the old prairies, the feathers in the Indian's hair would carry him up and set him down in the new world.

This Ghost Dance cult spread over many Indian Reservations. Some whites believed that it would cause Indians to start another uprising. They considered Sitting Bull a natural leader for such a rebellion.

Major James McLaughlin, Indian agent at Standing Rock, was ordered to arrest Sitting Bull. Forty Indian policemen then went to Sitting Bull's cabin on Grand River in South Dakota. Three of these young Indian policemen, Lieutenant Bull Head, Shave Head, and Red Tomahawk, found Sitting Bull asleep on the cabin floor and hustled him into his clothes.

Outside in the drizzly dawn, a group of Ghost Dancers surrounded them. Sitting Bull's son taunted his father for allowing the policemen to arrest him.

Seeing that the Ghost Dancers outnumbered the policemen, Sitting Bull screamed, "I will not go with you!"

Immediately, shots were fired. Shave Head and Bull Head fell, and Red Tomahawk shot the medicine man dead. Quickly, Red Tomahawk took charge and ordered all the policemen into the cabin for defense against the attacking Ghost Dancers. The Eighth Cavalry men now came over the hill to the rescue of the policemen.

While this happened at Standing Rock, troops had arrived at Pine Ridge, South Dakota, and many Indians there fled from the Reservation and off into the South Dakota Badlands. Here some of Sitting Bull's followers joined the band of Big Foot, a sick Miniconjou Sioux chief.

Troops arrived. Big Foot did not resist. Then the troops herded the Sioux into camp on Wounded Knee Creek. On December 29, 1890, soldiers searched the tepees for hidden guns. Someone fired a gun and the shameful Massacre of Wounded Knee began. When it was over, many Indian men, women, and children, and thirty soldiers lay dead.

The mighty Sioux had made their last stand when Yellow Hair met them upon the Greasy Grass. Their most famous leader, Sitting Bull, had been killed, not by whites but by another Indian. In the spring, no great earth-wave came to bury the whites and to bring back Uncle Buffalo and the ghosts from the dead.

146—Sitting Bull, the famous medicine man

147—Red Tomahawk

XI - The Builders

148—North Dakota's first capitol. The middle section was the Territorial capitol constructed in 1883.

1 - Flickertail State

Snow swirled over northern Dakota on May 14, 1889. Many residents rode to the polls in sleighs and voted for delegates to the Constitutional Convention. Northern Dakota had been divided into 25 districts of about equal population, each to provide three delegates.

Of the 75 persons elected to write the North Dakota constitution, 52 were native-born Americans; ten had come from Canada and 13 from European countries. Most were farmers, there being 29 of them. Lawyers ranked next with 25. Other delegates included 9 merchants, 5 bankers, 3 real estate dealers, 2 editors, one doctor and one railroad man.

They met at Bismarck on July 4 and took part in a gala parade. Troops from Fort Yates and from Fort Abraham Lincoln marched. Sitting Bull in a black suit and Rain-in-the-Face with an American flag over one ear joined Gall, Hairy Chin, John Grass, Mad Bear, Big Head and Strikes-the-Ree in the paleface procession. Girls on horseback represented the states of the Union.

149—North Dakota Senate in session, 1897

The delegates met in the House of Representatives assembly room. They debated several issues. Should women be allowed to vote? They finally decided that women could vote only in local school elections. Should they move the capital to another city? They decided against such removal. They adopted a state seal and the Australian ballot system. Should they allow the manufacture and sale of intoxicating liquors? They concluded that the people should vote on such a prohibition. Backers of the Louisiana State Lottery tried to install their lottery in North Dakota after it had been outlawed in their own state. The U. S. Congress eventually settled this hotly-debated issue when it made lottery groups illegal.

By Saturday, August 17, the delegates completed their work. Territorial Governor Mellette then called for an election on October 1.

Northern Dakotans adopted the Constitution by a vote of 27,441 to 8,107. Prohibition of alcoholic liquors carried by 1,159 votes.

150—Governor Lynn J. Frazier signs women's suffrage bill, 1917

President Benjamin Harrison on November 2, 1889, proclaimed North Dakota and South Dakota the 39th and 40th states in the Union. The next day John Miller took the oath of office as the first governor of the Flickertail State.

The first North Dakota legislature met on November 19 to select two men as U. S. Senators—Gilbert A. Pierce and Lyman R. Casey.

The lawmakers faced a lack of money. And North Dakota must pay its share of the Dakota Territory debts. Years of poor crops had slowed immigration into the state. Large areas of the western part of the state remained unsettled.

Of the thirteen public institutions provided by the new constitution, only three existed—the capitol, the state university at Grand Forks, and the hospital for the insane at Jamestown. But they managed to obtain $5000 for a school for the deaf to be erected at Devils Lake.

The state library was created in 1890 and was first maintained by the secretary of state. Many changes and much growth since, it now provides help in research and providing information to state officials and residents.

The early lawmakers established the Veterans' Home at Lisbon in 1893. On a 90-acre tract, this facility is now home for a maximum of 159 ambulant veterans, spouses, or surviving spouses.

2 - Sodbusters and Shanty Dwellers

The open-range rancher did not want homesteaders. Homesteaders would take from him the land on which he had raised cattle without buying the land or paying taxes on it. While the ranchers' Vigilantes did hunt down horse and cattle thieves, they also set fire to homesteaders' haystacks and damaged their property. The man with the lariat sneered at the man with the breaking plow and gave him such names as **honyocker, squatter, nestor,** or **sodbuster.**

But after the terrible winter of 1886-1887, most Dakota cattlemen quit and left the land to the oncoming homesteaders. When North Dakota became a state, farms covered the fertile Red River Valley, and homesteaders had taken claims along other streams and railways. But most of the treeless high prairies waited for landseekers. And so the second Great Dakota Boom of settlers flooded into North Dakota, beginning in 1898. Railroads continued advertising for settlers. The state legislature in 1905 allotted money for advertising the free land. Thousands of copies of The North Dakota Magazine, plus maps and wall posters sent to other states and to European countries spread news about the state's advantages. Homesteading continued in the northwestern part of the state until 1912.

151—Shanty on the prairie

152—Bachelor homesteader doing his laundry

153—A bachelor bakes bread in his claim shanty

154—Typical claim shanty

155—Interior of a lady homesteader's shanty

156—The sodbuster who made "good" often hired a photographer to take a picture of his new house and his family's "wheels." This he would send to his relatives in the Old Country to show how well he has done in the New World.

Immigrants from northern Europe and land-hungry Americans staked Dakota claims where there seemed to be little more than prairie and sky. But here was land, acres and acres to be claimed by anyone willing to live on it.

Some persons came with no intention of building a permanent home. For such people, staking a claim meant adventure, independence, an escape from a crowded city, or a free land grab they could sell later.

Few Flickertail State homesteaders came in covered wagons. Most took a train as close to unclaimed land as possible. Many a landseeker hired a liveryman, or a land locator, to show him the quarter sections of land still available. Once a man had decided what quarter section he wanted, he marked it to show it was being claimed. Then he went to the county seat, made application for that particular quarter section, and paid the $14 fee for filing. He would pay $4 more when he "proved up."

Homesteading laws changed over the years, but always a man must build a dwelling on the property and cultivate at least ten acres. He had to live on the claim for five years, though this was later reduced to three years.

And what sort of house could the homesteader build out where no trees grew?

A dugout in a hillside sheltered many a pioneer North Dakota family during its first years on the prairie. Most built sodhouses or tar-papered shanties.

For a sodhouse, a man spaded or plowed up strips of well-rooted sod. He cut the strips into 2- or 3-foot sections and laid the strips into walls about three feet thick. He built the sod walls around a log framework if he had access to a few trees. Otherwise, he simply built sod walls, putting in a framed door and a window or two. He covered the house with a roof of rough lumber laid over with heavy tarpaper, slough grass and sod, or perhaps shingles.

The sodhouse proved cool in the summer, warm in winter, and safe from prairie fires. Heavy rains, however, could soak through the roof. Mice easily came inside, so sodhouse dwellers prized a cat.

A frail shanty of rough pine boards sheltered hundreds of North Dakota homesteaders. The shanty dweller covered the outside walls and the roof with tarpaper held in place by laths. Newspapers, pasted layer upon layer on the inside walls, kept the wind—but not the cold—outside.

Few homesteaders owned a plow their first year on a claim. Breaking sod on those first ten acres cost from $2.50 to $5 per acre when it was hired done.

Flax became a common crop to plant the first year, though some farmers raised wheat or corn. Many homesteaders hauled grain by wagon or sled to a railway 30 to 40 miles away, camping overnight in the open air or spending the night with some hospitable homesteader along the way.

The first years on a claim, the homesteader without savings had to earn other than crop income in order to live. If bonepickers had not already gleaned the area, he gathered the bones of buffalo, and of cattle that had died during the terrible winter of 1886-1887. Many Dakota homesteading men went to Minnesota lumber camps to work during the winter months. Some trapped fur-bearing animals, or hunted coyotes and wolves on which there were bounties. Hundreds of pioneers snared gophers for a 3-cent bounty per tail. Railroad construction also offered employment.

To establish a profitable farm, the homesteader had to develop many skills. He learned to build of sod, or stone, or wood. He spaded a well, a cellar, or dugout stable, and learned to shoe horses or oxen, fix harnesses, even to tan a hide from which he could make harnesses. He made fences, learned to rope and brand cattle, to butcher a steer and dry, salt, or smoke its meat. He cleared his land of stone or sage or brush, hacked out lignite coal to fuel his stove. Many a homesteader built himself a stone-boat. This simple plank sledge drawn by a horse or an ox could glide over grass, mud, snow, or ice. When clearing land of stones and rocks, it served especially well and also was used for hauling manure out of a barn and onto fields. The pioneer North Dakotan had to learn farming methods that suited the prairie land and climate.

The sodbuster usually started out with a yoke of oxen to help him with field work. An ox could feed itself on the prairie grass and it cost less than a horse. A horse needed oats as well as hay and was easily stolen by a rustler.

When he had a job he could not do alone, Mr. Sodbuster found other homesteaders willing to help and exchange work. Together, homesteading neighbors constructed better barns, dug deeper wells, harvested crops, and organized the first township governments and rural school districts.

When Mr. Sodbuster went to town by wagon, he brought back mail and supplies for his neighbors as well as for himself. If darkness should overtake him on those trackless prairies, his yoke of oxen or team of horses would know the way home. Cheering lanterns glimmered over the prairies, for in early times many homesteaders hung a lighted lantern outside to guide a person to shelter in that sea of prairie grass. (A lantern covered with red cloth signaled something wrong and quickly brought neighbors.)

The terror of prairie fires the homesteader did not wait to experience—he plowed two or three circles of furrows around his farmstead. The grass growing within these circles he burned so that flying sparks from a fire could not ignite therein. He plowed firebreaks around his fields of ripening grain.

A prairie fire hurried along by wind could travel thirty miles an hour. Men, women, and children fought grass fires by flailing the flames with wet gunny sacks and old clothes.

It has been estimated that perhaps half of the men and women who came out to North Dakota to file on land never proved up to gain ownership. A dry summer, a blizzard or two, grasshoppers, the loneliness, and the boredom of doing little or nothing soon separated the squatter from the man willing to work hard for his future. A sort of "survival of the fittest" left on the prairie the strong-hearted and cheerful, the workers who did the actual building of the Flickertail State.

3 - *Around the Town Pump*

In homesteading years there existed post offices that were little more than a name, a home to which neighboring homesteaders could walk to get their mail. Sometimes this home "post master" added supplies which he sold.

Usually a town began next to a railway. A man would set up a general store. Settlers rode or drove in with horses to get supplies, and the storekeeper added a hitching rail outside his store to which customers could tie their horses. The storekeeper and his family needed water, so he dug a well—and put a watering trough alongside for customers' horses.

For a while, the storekeeper and his family lived in a back room of the store. Then as business prospered, he built a house. By this time a blacksmith might put up a shop alongside the store and that way Main Street began. Homesteaders brought in their horses—even oxen—to have them shod, and the blacksmith sharpened plow lays and made tools as more sod was turned into fields.

Next, a grain warehouse appeared alongside the railway tracks. Much smaller than the grain elevators of later years, it was a building where homesteaders could unload their grain sacks for rail shipment. The railway added a station, and with more people coming either to visit relatives or to do business, a small frame hotel became the young town's next building.

Everyone in the little town fetched water from the storekeeper's well. The pump became the place where you met and chatted with neighbors.

People who came on the train needed a way to get where they wanted to go, so some ambitious man built a livery barn. Here one could rent a horse to ride, or a buggy, or a buckboard, or a wagon. Farmers coming a distance with a load of grain could rent a stall overnight for their horses, and a room for themselves in the frame hotel. At first, the hotel usually served food for their roomers—no choice in the menu. Soon, however, a man whose wife was an ambitious cook, opened a restaurant.

During this time, the storekeeper had a small post office corner in his building where he sorted the mail. But as the community became better settled, a postmaster was appointed for the town and the post office was added to the row of buildings on Main Street.

With each new business, there usually came a family and for each family a house. Some families built a small barn nearby for a cow so they could have their own supply of fresh milk. A flock of chickens often shared that barn and provided fresh eggs for the family.

Children must go to school, and so the first white frame schoolhouse was built—always with a bell tower. While in the early years, folks held worship services in their houses, many used the schoolhouse once it was available. Eventually, a congregation built its first church—each with a steeple and bell.

Early settlers found a plentiful supply of "prairie chickens" to help with their food supply, and while most farmers learned to butcher livestock for their own use, townspeople were happy to have a butcher establish his shop. He bought cattle, hogs, and chickens from farmers and prepared meat for his town customers.

After several years of good crops, and evidence of another prosperous farming community, a regular grain elevator took the place of the little grain warehouse alongside the railroad.

Refrigerators and freezers did not then exist, so some settlers cut ice from a nearby stream and stored this in saw dust in an outdoor cellar. In town a man might start an ice business, storing large ice blocks in his ice warehouse. Folks in town bought ice from him for their ice boxes.

Nearby farmers might haul milk, cream, and butter to town to trade for groceries or to sell to people in town. Peddlers made their rounds in town and in the country selling everything from kitchen utensils, parlor organs, patent medicines, to Watkins products.

In the early years, if a fire got started, the only fire fighting apparatus was a bucket brigade from the nearest pump. Then when a water tower took the place of the town pump, fire departments purchased a hose cart drawn by men or horses.

As folks found their town growing, they began to think of more entertainment besides the games and dances they enjoyed in their homes or at the schoolhouse. So they built what they called the opera house. This was not elegant like a real opera house in large cities, but it provided a place where traveling musicians, actors, and vaudeville groups could entertain.

Pool halls were built for men only. No respectable lady ever went into a pool hall or saloon. A confectionery was a place with fancy tables and chairs where ladies and gentlemen could be served ice cream or sodas or candy, cookies and cake, or **sarsaparilla**.

The earliest newspapers in a community were mostly for printing legal notices of homestead filings and land claims. Many such newspapers moved

157—Beginning of a pioneer town (Flasher), 1905

once homesteading had been completed in an area. A few remained to become newspapers for printing news and selling advertisements and so a newspaper office was added to Main Street.

Just as post offices had first been established to accommodate homesteaders on foot, so the first towns were built to accommodate farmers who came to town by horse, buggy, or wagon. Then along came the horseless carriage that would change buildings and life in town and on the farm.

Automobiles needed gasoline, so gasoline pumps were installed in the larger towns first. In those days, each auto driver must be his own mechanic. Then the most logical place to get help with auto repair was the blacksmith shop. As the blacksmith learned more and more about cars, he did less and less blacksmithing and more and more auto repair. So the auto garage gradually took the place of the blacksmith shop—and here cars could be sold and repaired.

About this time another new contraption came to town. It was the moving picture machine. The practical place for showing moving pictures was the opera house. Gradually the opera house became the movie house.

After World War I, the livery stable—and the little barns behind houses—gradually disappeared as folks sold their horses and bought a car instead. Hitching rails disappeared along Main Street. Concrete sidewalks took the place of board walks. Dirt streets that had been good enough for horses were replaced by hard-surface streets.

The marvel of electric power brought street lights. Refrigerators put the ice man out of business. Folks no longer needed to keep a cow and chickens. The butcher shop disappeared as meat departments became part of grocery stores turned into supermarkets. The old general store gave way to special kinds of stores. Motels more convenient for auto drivers replaced aging hotels.

And so the town familiar to the horse-driving homesteader changed to a town he would not recognize. Many of the smaller towns would eventually disappear so that today only a few buildings remain, perhaps none at all—only a crumbling foundation. With the automobile taking the place of the horse, people could travel greater distances in less time. Folks drove to larger cities to shop where stores were larger and had a greater variety of goods, usually at lower prices. The village and small home town stores would lose so much business they would have to close. The hard times of the Twenties, the depression and drouth of the Thirties and the need for defense workers in World War II caused thousands of people to leave North Dakota towns and farms. Buses made it possible to transport children and this brought about school consolidations; that brought the closing of schools in the smaller villages as well as one-room schools in the country.

158—Cutting blocks of ice for storage

159—Interior of an early general store, 1902

160—A harness shop at Belfield, 1912

4 - Pioneer Society

In the horse-and-buggy days, people seldom went far from the home community. Breadwinners worked many hours each day. Most little towns adjusted store hours to suit the customer— general stores sometimes staying open until ten at night. The village housewife did not yet have electric labor-saving devices, so she gave much time and energy to household chores. Frugal women sewed clothes, particularly for themselves, their daughters and small children, sewing by hand or with a treadle sewing machine.

Parents and children worked together to produce at home not only food and clothing, but fun as well. Young people customarily learned to play stringed musical instruments. They brought such instruments along to picnics and gatherings and they organized different musical groups.

At many evening get-togethers in homes, women tatted, embroidered, or knitted while they visited. They had quilting bees. The young folks played games that needed little or no equipment. People made their own fun, enjoyed taffy pulls and singing rounds. Local magicians showed their friends their "magic." During winter months particularly, prairie townsfolk seldom depended on any kind of commercial entertainment.

In the larger North Dakota cities of that time there developed the "silk-stockinged set." These were the families of the wealthier men in the city. Their wives dressed in silks, satins, velvets, brocades, furs, and jewels. Dresses, coats, capes, mufflers, gloves, and hats were fancy and greatly ornamented. Spangles, beads, silk fringes, chiffons, ribbons, and laces were used for trimmings. Women forced themselves into tight whale-bone corsets. They carried dainty parasols and they liked jeweled, hand-painted or richly-embroidered accessories. The "silk-stockinged" ladies hired a dressmaker to sew their clothes; they went to a millinery shop where ostrich-plumed and beribboned hats were put together for them.

The houses of the "well to do" were large and much decorated. They had large porches, towers, and "gingerbread" ornamentation on gables outside; inside, carved woodwork, perhaps floors with inlaid designs, elegant furniture, lace curtains, statuary, family photographs and oil paintings hanging high in fancy frames.

Young girls in such homes took lessons in proper speaking, how to gesture and walk gracefully. At sixteen a girl put on long skirts, and at the same age a boy would graduate from knee knickers to long pants.

Labor was cheap. The rich women hired at least one maid to do the housework, perhaps also some-one to do the cooking and baking, another the laundry. Immigrant women usually found their first employment as "hired girls" in private homes, earning little more than their board and room.

Amateur actors performed in many prairie towns. Spelling bees, declamations, and debate societies entertained homesteader folks.

County and local fairs served as a place where farm families met friends. Prizes for the best farm products exhibited were agricultural books and pamphlets. In these early fairs, education came first and entertainment second. For entertainment there were usually plowing matches, children's foot races, athletic contests, some horse races, and always a baseball game. Eventually, carnival entertainment was added to a fair, and soon the farmer's family spent more time riding the Ferris wheel and the merry-go-round, and watching the sword-swallower and the fire-eater than they did at the agricultural exhibits.

Baseball held first place for summer entertainment. Intense rivalries developed between prairie town baseball teams. Games were, of course, played afternoons.

The first football team was organized at the North Dakota Agricultural College, Fargo, in 1893. The first basketball team in the state organized at the Fargo YMCA in the winter of 1895-96.

On river ice, lacrosse and curling, skating, hockey, and racing horses (specially shod) provided winter sport. Bicycle and harness racing took place at many county fairs. Auto racing began shortly after 1900.

Wrestling and boxing sometimes entertained followers in baseball parks or in the opera houses. Trapshooting, checkers, and chess had many players.

For the homesteader family out on a farm, life held far more labor than recreation The distances from neighbors made rural folks appreciate company, whether that of stranger or friend. Any person who stopped at a homestead would be welcomed, invited for a meal or to stay for the night. Homesteader children often slept on the floor in order to give their bed to visitors.

Prairie children lacked play equipment, but they had great fun in games of running, jumping, and hiding. Winter or summer, they played outside with neighbor children. Grownups gathered in their small houses to dance, to play cards, or just for the pleasure of talking with one another. Once a farmer had become so prosperous as to have a barn with a hay loft, that hay loft often became the scene of barn dances. Accordions and fiddles supplied the music for quick-stepping men in overalls and women in calico and gingham.

In the wee hours of morning, such neighbors returned to houses they never locked, caught a few hours of sleep, then got up for another day of labor.

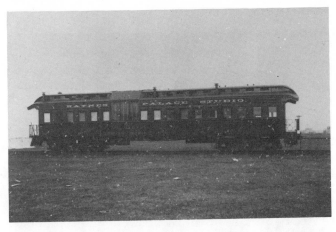

161—Hundreds of homesteaders had their pictures taken when this traveling Haynes studio car stopped at a town.

164—Hunting party at Lostwood

162—Folks gather for a celebration in a pioneer town, 1905

165—Kirkwood Hotel at Carrington

163—Quilting bees were popular during North Dakota's early years

166—The opera house at Wahpeton

167—From the author's collection of immigrant homesteader photographs. Such pictures were sent to relatives and friends left behind in the Old Country.

Story of the Peace Garden State, page 94

This was long before permanent press and fabric softeners. Women sewed their own clothes or hired a seamstress, and a tailor made suits for men.

5 - Prairie Wheels

North Dakota became a state in the horse-and-buggy days. The squealing Red River Carts had vanished. A few stagecoaches operated. The last grain-carrying steamers were making short trips on the Red River. A small number of lumber and wheat boats plied the Missouri. Commercial transportation depended chiefly on railways which now criss-crossed the state, with more feeder lines building each year into new farming areas.

To go beyond a railway station, one traveled by horse- and-buggy, in a stagecoach, in a rumbling wagon, or on horseback. Sometimes one even had to ride a stoneboat to one's destination. This simple plank sled skimmed over mud where wheels sank to their hubs, and it could also slide over snow too deep for a sleigh.

In the larger towns of early North Dakota, traffic regulations prohibited driving a horse and buggy faster than 8 miles an hour. To trot a horse across a bridge was unlawful. One man drove a steam engine down a Fargo street and he was fined $5 for frightening horses along the way. Anyone who rode an unlighted bicycle after dark would be fined $5.

Many train carloads of bicycles were shipped into North Dakota during the 1890s because "wheeling" was then the most common way to travel. A person who could not afford a horse and carriage could afford a "wheel." Bicycle clubs were popular. Young people went bicycling together, and police wheeled after lawbreakers.

Then came the horseless carriage. The very first automobile driven in North Dakota had been manufactured in Germany. It belonged to a Saint Paul business, and it arrived in Grand Forks on June 28, 1897, and was driven around town to advertise Carnation cigars.

In 1900 two Fargo businessmen each bought a one-cylinder Oldsmobile and on the Fourth of July they got ready for the first automobile race in North Dakota. Just as they were about to start west on Front Street, in Fargo, a Minneapolis man drove up in his two-cylinder Cadillac. The three cars lined up, and at the sound of the starting gun they streaked off in a cloud of dust. The Cadillac took early lead but lost its way. Banker R. S. Lewis skidded around a corner at 20 miles an hour and landed on a boulevard. But he took fresh grip on his steering bar and finally passed C. S. Barnes, Fargo's first garageman.

In a state where long distances often separated farms and ranches, North Dakotans soon took interest in the possible uses of the horseless carriage. Many different persons and companies then manufactured autos. Such autos were really not much more than a buggy with a motor added to turn the wheels. So numbers of North Dakotans set about making their own horseless carriages.

In 1900 O. A. Beeman purchased a four-and-one-half horsepower engine and built a four-passenger vehicle at Valley City. He took friends on several jaunts and his sputtering vehicle so frightened a team of horses that they ran away and smashed the buggy. That was the first "auto accident" in North Dakota.

Later the Fargo mayor asked Beeman to drive his auto to Fargo and take part in a festival parade there. Beeman did so, and folks paid 25 cents each for a ride in his horseless carriage.

That same year Brown's Bicycle Store in Fargo ordered a Locomobile steam car, and another Fargoan ordered an electric runabout. When such cars were driven about Fargo— or to other nearby towns— people stopped whatever they were doing and stared at these strange contraptions. Children ran down the streets, following excitedly after. Newspapers published stories about the automobiles and their drivers' experiences with them.

At the turn of the century, there were 135 automobile manufacturers in the United States. Most of these made gasoline-fueled vehicles as these were proving more practical than the steam and electric cars.

In North Dakota automobiles had to travel the dirt roads over which horses could easily go. One car built especially for country roads had high wheels and was called the Buckmobile. Mud plagued the early automobiles, so driving horseless carriages was done only during nice weather.

By 1905 cars had become common enough in North Dakota cities and towns that the legislature passed its first law concerning autmobiles. That law set a speed limit of 8 miles per hour in cities and villages, 15 miles in the country. A gasoline automobile must be equipped with a horn or a bell which the driver must sound at least 15 rods behind any horse-drawn vehicle it approached. "Autoists" must come to a stop if the driver of a horse-drawn vehicle so signaled.

In 1911 cars had so increased in the state that the legislature passed its first licensing law, instituting a fee of $3 for each car. There were 7,220 cars registered that year. By this time people had decided it was better to buy than to make your own automobile.

As the gasoline-fueled automobiles showed they could be driven long distances, automobile tours became common. Four teenagers made the news when they drove a Moline Dreadnaught Touring from Astoria, Illinois, across North Dakota to Red Lodge, Montana in the summer of 1911.

Since gasoline stations had not yet been installed, they purchased their gasoline at grocery and hardware stores, paying 12 cents per gallon. At Bismarck, they had to cross the Missouri on a ferry, and the ferryboat operator was puzzled about what fee to charge them. All fees up to that time had been per horse and per person. Finally, he decided that 25 cents would be a fair fee.

168—Homemade auto, about 1910, New England

171—Touring car at Hettinger, about 1910

169—Earl Branick's homemade hot rod, 1908

172—A 1912 Brush runabout

170—Ole Rosholt drives his first runabout

173—Early touring car. Lady passenger wears a "duster."

174—The automobile, unable to travel wherever horses could go, necessitated the building of hard-surface roads.

175—Where streams were too deep to ford, a ferry transported vehicles. This one was Challoner's Ferry on the Little Missouri in McKenzie County.

176—McLean County road-building outfit, early 1920s

Three years later North Dakota ranked fifth in the nation in automobiles per capita. Most roads then were only tracks made by wagons and buggies whose horsepower could pull them up hills which the horseless carriages could not climb. As late as World War I, car drivers avoided long or steep hills. Since these automobiles had no fuel pumps, they depended on a gravity supply of fuel. To climb a hill in reverse became the usual thing to do, for then the gasoline tank under the driver's seat became higher than the motor.

So the automobile encouraged the building of better roads. Wagon roads with ruts a foot deep did not trouble horse and buggy, but the low-axled cars could not travel such.

The earliest highway in North Dakota was just a trail; it led from the Mandan earthlodge villages, past Dog Den Butte, along the west side of the Turtle Mountains and on to the trading posts in Canada. A Red River Cartway crossed the Red River near presentday Wahpeton and took a route west of the river to Pembina and Fort Garry (Winnipeg). Supply wagons to military posts, stage coaches, and freight haulers left rutted trails over the prairies.

Stage coach service first reached Fort Abercrombie from St. Cloud, Minnesota, in 1859. One of the earliest stage coach routes led up the Red River Valley to Winnipeg. The Black Hills gold rush brought hundreds of people traveling by stagecoach from Bismarck to Deadwood plus wagons carrying freight.

As the railroads spread over North Dakota, horse-drawn wagons carried freight out to various towns not reached by rail. Such stage coaches and drays continued operating until motor trucks and buses replaced them.

Before fences had been built, settlers traveled cross country, going around sloughs and lakes, fording streams where possible, and driving around hills. In 1899 the legislature declared all section lines reserved for public roads. Roads could use the width of two rods on each side of a section line. Thus began North Dakota's grid pattern of roads.

During the first thirty years of statehood, townships and counties were responsible for any road building. To finance local road or bridge building, male residents paid an annual poll tax of $1.50. Or, instead of paying the tax, they could work one day repairing or improving a road.

The 1913 legislature created the first state highway commission. Federal aid for roads began in 1916 and the following year 3,768 miles were made state highways. Road and bridge building increased during the 1920s, but the greatest advance came after World War II. In 1945 the state had only 1,600 miles of hard-surfaced roads; by 1960 it had over 5,000. Construction of the National Interstate highways began in North Dakota in 1958 and were completed in 1977. North Dakota was the first state to complete its Interstate. By 1990 the number of hard-surfaced roads in the state totaled 14,506 miles; there were 1,045 miles of 4-lane highways, and 92,106 of dirt and gravel roads. The Motor Vehicle Department had registered over 370,000 automobiles in 1989, more than 200,000 trucks, nearly 42,000 farm trucks and 22,000 motorcycles.

6 - Skyways

Seven years after the Wright brothers proved that man can fly, Archie Hoxey made the first airplane flight in North Dakota. At Grand Forks, Hoxey, who had flown with the Wrights, took Frank Kent up as the first airplane passenger.

Though Hoxey made the first flight from North Dakota soil, he did not bring the first "aeroplane" into the state. Two years earlier, in 1908, a Minot man, Dewey Dorman, sent for a flying machine that cost him $4,500. He had never operated an airplane, but he had driven automobiles, and in those days driving an automobile was considered as risky as flying. So when his flying machine arrived at the Minot depot, Dewey loaded it onto a dray and took it to a big hill south of Minot.

He decked himself out in flying clothes and goggles, for he had already promised to do some flying for the Ward County Fair. A large crowd gathered to see Dewey Dorman take off, but the wind blew so hard he decided to stay on the ground.

Next day, with perfect weather, Dewey whirled the propeller, taxied around a few times, then soared 4 feet off the ground before postponing further flight.

A couple months later, having gathered enough nerve to fly up into the clouds, Dewey invited friends to observe the epoch flight. But this time when the motor started, the flying machine caught on fire. Dewey and his friends shoved the thing into the Souris River, and that was the end of North Dakota's first plane.

More successful was North Dakota's first aviator, Tom McGoey of Grand Forks. He built his own Curtiss type flying machine, mounting the 8-cylinder engine in the rear. He perched an ordinary chair seat on a swivel, and thus from his "cockpit" McGoey helped balance the plane by tilting himself forward or backward, to the right or to the left! A steering stick pushed forward inclined the airplane front upwards. Pulled back, it elevated the ship. Cables connected the rudder to this steering apparatus.

In this dangerous craft, McGoey made his first flight from the Grand Forks fairgrounds on July 12, 1911. He stayed in the air 15 minutes. During the next three months he barnstormed as far away as Michigan, at one time going up 1,500 feet. (To barnstorm meant touring the country, giving short airplane rides, and doing stunt flying.) But after

177—Crowds gathered to celebrate the dedication of the Verendrye Memorial bridge over the Missouri at Sanish, 1927.

178—Thomas McGoey at the controls of the plane he had built

179—McGoey's plane in flight

nearly killing himself, McGoey returned to Grand Forks where he worked as an electrician until his death in 1938.

Following the first World War, many young air force pilots returned home, the flying fever in their blood, eager to go barnstorming, anything to give them a livelihood as flyers. In those years, fairgoers thrilled to aerial acrobats walking plane wings, sliding back to ride the airplane tail, hanging from a rope, standing on a wing during loops, changing from one plane to another in flight, or from a racing automobile to a plane.

Among these was a Fargoan, Vern Roberts, who flew a canvas-winged "Jenny" at many exhibits in the state. Like other early aviators, Roberts had some spine-tingling adventures. He once flew into the center of a tornado and was tossed up to 20,000 feet. But he landed with only minor damage to his plane.

North Dakota's first woman pilot was Florence "Tree Tops" Klingensmith. She attained national fame as a racer and stunt flyer. In a machine purchased for her by Fargo business men, Tree Tops looped her plane 143 times over Hector Airport. The next year, at Minneapolis, she set an official world record of 1,078 turns. But in 1933 during a race at Chicago, she plunged to her death when her ship's wings weakened at 200 miles an hour.

The ace of early North Dakota flyers was Carl Ben Eielson of Hatton. Home from the army air force, he and his friends bought a Flying Jenny which Ben paid for by barnstorming. Then, for his worried father's sake, Ben went to Alaska to teach school and forget about flying. But he talked flying to his English students and to the townspeople of Fairbanks until his friends there bought another canvas-winged Jenny for Ben to fly. He thrilled Alaskans with his stunts, began carrying miners and doctors to remote areas, thus saving them days and weeks of slow travel. He flew the first air mail in Alaska. He was the first man to fly in the Arctic winter, the first to land a wheeled plane on snow and on the frozen Arctic sea.

As pilot for Hubert Wilkins, he flew over the roof of the world in a 2,200-mile nonstop flight from Pt. Barrow, Alaska, to Green Harbour, Spitzbergen, April 16, 1928. He helped explore the Antarctic by plane.

Then he flew to his death on a rescue flight to a fur-trading ship frozen into the ice off Siberia. Thousands mourned the death of this modest young man who had become North Dakota's hero. A majestic snow-crowned mountain in Alaska, the great air force base outside Fairbanks, and schools and an air force base in North Dakota are named for Carl Ben Eielson.

A North Dakota farmer, E. M. Canfield, did his courting in an airplane, then taught his bride how to fly. The two became widely known as the Flying

180—Carl Ben Eielson

Canfields. Besides operating a flying circus for community gatherings, the Canfields pioneered the hunting of coyotes by plane.

The plane which first came to North Dakota as a novelty is now employed in passenger, express, and mail service. It has also been used for weed and insect control. In 1989 the Aeronautics Commission registered a total of 1,795 aircraft in North Dakota.

7 - "News Walkers"

The earliest regular system of communication on the North Dakota prairies was that of the Indian "news walker." This brave traveled from band to band, telling the news he gathered as he visited each village. A hardy man, the news walker always went on foot no matter what the weather or the season. News has since been delivered different ways by the palefaces.

Pembina became the first post office in North Dakota when Norman Kittson was appointed its postmaster in 1849. Metis men who could neither read nor write carried the letters and newspapers. They traveled on foot, horseback, cart, canoe - any way they could get between Pembina and Crow Wing, Minnesota.

Other hardy men carried the first mail into North Dakota from Fort Abercrombie when they delivered to Sibley's soldiers in the summer of 1863. Fort Rice, on the Missouri, got its mail by steamboat. Sometimes in winter months a brave man carried the post between Fort Rice and lower Missouri River forts by sneaking through the willow thickets along the river bottoms. When Fort Stevenson and Fort Totten were established, soldiers and civilians as well as friendly Indians carried official dispatches and mail on foot or by horse between the forts. Palmer's Spring Park near Fort Totten commemorates the place where three soldiers died while defending a government mail wagon in 1868.

As settlers came into the country, mail first reached them now and then by steamer, horse, or stagecoach. Regular mail delivery was first established between towns. Delivery to rural patrons, first by horse and buggy, developed most after the advent of the automobile.

181—Ryder News office, 1935

The earliest northern Dakota newspaper appeared at Fort Union in July of 1864. Four issues of this **Frontier Scout** were published by two Wisconsin men, Robert Winegar and Ira F. Goodwin. The following year, **Frontier Scout** appeared at Fort Rice, this time edited by Captain E. G. Adams. It apparently had been run off the same printing press used at Fort Union.

Many presses came into Dakota Territory with townsite boomers and wherever a settlement of homesteaders began. First issues of these handset newspapers were often printed in a tent.

Few of these publications operated to publish news. Most presses depended for income on the printing of official homestead notices.

After 1879 every homesteader was required by law to publish a final-proof notice of his claim in five consecutive issues of the newspaper located nearest to his land. Fees for printing homestead claims ranged from $5 to $6.50 each. Some newspapers carried over 200 such notices in a single issue.

Hundreds of this kind of newspapers prospered in Dakota during the homesteading era. Then as soon as a vicinity was settled and the final notices concluded, the printer and his press moved to another locality about to be settled. Only a few of these presses remained in a community to become a small town weekly.

Colonel Clement A. Lounsberry established the first regular newspaper in North Dakota in 1873. The first train into Bismarck brought the press for this **Bismarck Tribune**. Three years later, Lounsberry made the greatest newspaper "scoop" in North Dakota's history when he reported the Custer Massacre to the nation.

The Fargo **Express** began operating on January 1, 1874. The Grand Forks **Plain Dealer** appeared the same year. Goldie West worked as managing editor of the Fargo **Argus**, another early newspaper, and he used railroad spikes and a six shooter to

weight papers on his desk. For printing his boom edition, he powered his press with a threshing rig's steam engine belting in power from the street.

Because of the large number of Norwegians settling in the state, the papers with the biggest circulation in North Dakota during early statehood were the Norwegian language papers, the Fargo **Fram** and the Grand Forks **Normanden**.

The first telegraph line reached Fargo in 1871 and continued up the Red River Valley that same year to Pembina and Winnipeg, Canada. But who installed the first telephone in North Dakota is not certain.

When Alexander Graham Bell displayed his new invention at the Philadelphia Exposition in 1876, others beside the Emperor of Brazil recognized the possibilities of the telephone. Bonanza wheat farmers from the Red River Valley could see its practical use in connecting subdivision farms with headquarters. J. L. Grandin bought telephone apparatus and installed a system on his farms in Traill Couuty. Oliver Dalrymple also purchased equipment from Mr. Bell and installed telephones on his farms near Casselton.

The first commercial telephone in the world was, supposedly, established in Massachusetts as early as April of 1877. Pioneer Traill County residents insisted that the Grandin Farms used telephones before that time.

M. M. Borman installed the earliest dial telephones in North Dakota at Abercrombie about 1900. That was 38 years before the dial system was first put into public use in the state.

First telephone switchboard in the state opened for business in the attic of Headquarters Hotel in Fargo on June 7, 1881, with fifteen-year old Bella Thomson as operator. At Bismarck that same year,

C. E. V. Draper connected the Bismarck Hotel and the Franklin Hotel with a telephone. A few years later, he built the first telephone system in the Bismarck-Mandan community. In 1885 a telephone line reached out to the store of "King John" Satterlund at Washburn. This first long distance line in North Dakota "worked some of the time."

Pictures, like the written word, serve communication. It was a farmer at Hunter who made it possible for the average person to take pictures. In his cyclone cellar, David Henderson Houston invented the Kodak, the first camera to handle roll film. Houston patented this camera in 1881 and sold manufacturing rights to the Eastman Company.

While Houston operated his farm at Hunter, young Frank Jay Haynes set up a studio at Fargo. He left this studio occasionally to take photographing trips that have left us a rich heritage of historical pictures. He went by stagecoach to Bismarck and Deadwood, by steamer to Fort Benton and return to Bismarck on a flat boat. The year Houston patented his Kodak, Haynes explored Yellowstone National Park to make stereoscopic views. When the Northern Pacific's final spike was driven near Garrison, Montana, Haynes was there to photograph the event. He outfitted a railway car as his traveling studio, stopping in railway towns where folks could come aboard the studio to have their pictures taken. He became the official photographer for the Northern Pacific Railway as well as for the Yellowstone National Park.

When radio crystal sets crackled with static and you heard only through earphones, hundreds of Americans put together broadcasting sets and had fun operating them. A few North Dakotans were experimenting with such amateur outfits before World War I.

The first commercial broadcasting station in the state opened in a small room in the tower of the Cass County courthouse in Fargo on May 22, 1922. WDAY's first "studio" contained the 50-watt broadcasting set, three chairs, a Victrola phonograph, a table, and three men—Kenneth Hance, Lawrence Hamm, and Earl C. Reincke.

After a year of competing with the tower's chimes and sparrows, WDAY moved to a new location above the Topic Cigar Store. Here the staff added a piano and swathed the room with heavy drapery. On top of the building they erected a 30-foot antenna. Their programs reached as far as Hillsboro.

Second broadcasting station to be licensed in the state was Wahpeton's WMAW which ceased after two years. Other early radio stations included KFYR at Bismarck, KDLR at Devils Lake, KCCU at Mandan, and KLPM at Minot. When KFYR built its 704-foot tower near Menoken in 1939 this was the highest tower of its kind in the world.

Many improvements have been made in radio since these first North Dakota stations began operating. Radios were entertainment novelties in the beginning, but they soon proved valuable to business as a medium of advertising. Radio stations sprang up all over the state, adding local public announcements and weather forecasts to their fare of entertainment and advertising. By 1990 there were 68 radio stations in the state.

North Dakota's pioneer television station at Minot began its first telecasts in June, 1952, over a closed circuit to several business places and a few homes. It went on the air as a regular commercial station on Easter Sunday, April 4, 1953.

For most of its fare the early years, KCJB-TV (now known as KXMC-TV) had to depend on local programs. Teenagers, ministers, and parents put on programs. Members of the university staff at Fargo came once weekly to produce an educational series. Local actors had fun with a hillbilly show. County agents provided 4-H demonstrations. Live telecasts were made of local sports and of the state fair.

Cis Hadley, North Dakota's first woman on television, produced shows regularly. And there was "Arv's Kitchen" in which the star performers were Arv Johnson, the announcer, and Harry Burris, rector of Minot's All Saints' Episcopal Church.

The evening's cooking demonstration on Arv's Kitchen once called for baked potatoes stuffed with cheese. Arv had read somewhere that one could drill a hole in a spud with an apple corer, then stuff the hole with cheese—and bake. Well, the potatoes began baking, but the cheese melted all over the oven, and smoke billowed about the tiny studio. Viewers called in to ask why their pictures were suddenly foggy. Jim Adelson, the sports announcer, tossed a pair of leather gloves across the studio to Arv who was trying to get the potatoes out of the oven. Arv snatched five potatoes out of the oven, then shut the door on the smoking ruin.

Shortly a man called long distance from Westhope. "Tell Arv," he said, "that he put six potatoes in there. He took out only five. There's still one in there burning."

Smoking potatoes doubtless do not trouble the 25 television stations which now broadcast from cities in North Dakota.

8 - Book Learning

When North Dakota entered the Union in 1889, there were 1,362 elementary schools operating. Half a dozen of these were graded schools in the larger towns, and there appear to have been six high schools in existence.

The first school in North Dakota was taught at Pembina by a Catholic missionary, Father Dumoulin, in 1818. He held classes in his own home. When he found that the mission and school were in U. S. territory, he returned to Canada and his church and school were abandoned in 1823.

The first public school building in the state was built at Pembina in 1876. Minnesota lumber came to Moorhead by rail, then was shipped by steamer as far as Goose Rapids on the Red River, and hauled the rest of the way by horses. Pembina children studied in this schoolhouse until 1881. It is now preserved by the local Masonic Lodge.

The first public school, however, may have started at Caledonia in 1872. About this time other schools opened in towns reached by the railway.

The North Dakota superintendent of public instruction in 1890 found there were 1,470 schools in the state. Of these, two were sod shanties, 40 were of log. Seventeen city schools boasted brick structures, and there were 1,391 frame buildings. The rest of the schools had no buildings but met in private homes. One teacher taught in a sod house where the family kept to one side while she gathered her pupils around the table. During one winter day a hen with frosted legs clucked gratefully under the table, and a sick pig lay in a box beside the stove.

Sixteen of those schoolhouses in 1890 had no blackboard. Fifty-one had no privy, 253 had only one. Over 300 schools got along without a dictionary. Forty-three boasted a small library of books. The total number of school library books in the entire state that first year amounted to 2,058.

The 38,000 children living in the new state did not all hurry off to school each day. Even after the state legislature passed a law requiring children to attend, many farm boys and girls stayed home whenever there was work that needed them. Some quit school altogether as soon as their parents thought they had learned enough reading and writing.

As late as 1918 only 54 percent of the pupils who started first grade came for the second grade. About one out of every four pupils finished eighth grade. Less than two percent completed high school.

About half of the teachers during the first ten years of statehood taught without certificates. Among homesteaders, any person who had completed more grades than anyone else in the neighborhood was elected to teach the local school. Teen-age girls taught on permits when adult teachers were not to be found. Adults earned short-term certificates by passing a county superintendent's examination.

Because many communities in North Dakota had a large number of immigrants, grownup newcomers often came to school to learn to speak and read English. Sometimes a mail-order catalog served the newcomer as a "reader" for learning English words. Because in many pioneer communities school was often held for only a few months during the year, many pupils could not make a grade each year. So it was not unusual for teenage boys and girls to be in the fourth, fifth, or sixth grades.

182—Drawing of first schoolhouse (center) at Pembina, 1818

183—North Dakota's first frame public schoolhouse, Pembina, 1876

184—Rural school near Hatton, 1898

185—Tar-papered rural school, Williams County, in use from 1903 to 1913

186—Lunch time in a one-room school during the Thirties

For many years the North Dakota rural teacher went to school early on fall and winter mornings in order to build a fire of wood or revive one burning lignite coal. In pioneer times, school was not held in winter months, but only for three or six months during warm weather.

Basket or pie socials raised money for buying story books, a treadle organ, a globe to hang from the ceiling, or a water fountain to take the place of the water bucket and dipper.

At the end of the school term, parents and pupils gathered at a tree grove or at the schoolhouse to celebrate with a picnic. The teacher returned home or took another school. Often, she married one of the bachelors in the school district. Few rural "schoolmarms" taught more than two or three years.

In the first decade of statehood, a teacher's salary was usually under $40 a month. She did not pay for board and room, but stayed at each pupil's home in turn, often sharing a bed with the girls of the family.

A Presbyterian college which opened at Jamestown in 1886 was the first to offer teacher training in the state. The depression of 1893 closed Jamestown College and its building stood vacant for years. Pigeons and sparrows flew through broken windows and nested inside until young Barend Kroeze in 1907 came and reopened the college.

A Congregational school, Fargo College, began operation in 1890. Fargo College had opened in rented quarters, then moved to its first building on the hill south of Island Park. Lack of money closed it in 1922.

North Dakota Methodists established Red River Valley University at Wahpeton in 1891. After operating for twelve years, it joined with the University of North Dakota at Grand Forks and became Wesley College.

In 1886, a Baptist "university" opened at Tower City, but soon closed for need of money. Afterwards, a Baptist college had a short life at Lisbon. Northwestern College existed briefly at Velva. At Portland, a Lutheran school first known as Portland Normal School and Business College, opened its doors in the fall of 1890; later, it continued as Bruflat Academy. In 1918, it merged with Concordia College at Moorhead, Minnesota.

A Roman Catholic school offering courses for upper grades, high school, and two years of college opened at Devils Lake in 1896. This St. Gall's College operated until 1903. The Benedictine monks then moved to Richardton and operated a similar school, St. Mary's College, from 1899 to 1924. Four years later, the school re-opened as Assumption College; it closed in 1974.

The state constitution in 1889 provided for a "scientific college" to be located at Wahpeton. The North Dakota State College of Science opened in 1903 in the Red River Valley University building. It is the second largest continuously operating junior college in the United State.

In 1890 the state legislature voted to establish a school for the deaf at Devils Lake. For the first two years citizens of the city furnished free a frame building for the first deaf children. Then the Great Northern Railroad donated an 18-acre tract of land a mile north of the city and the first building, "Old Main," was constructed in 1892.

The Grafton State School (now State Developmental Center) opened in 1904. It cares for and trains for work opportunities persons with developmental disabilities.

The North Dakota School for the Blind was first established at Bathgate in 1908. It moved to a new facility in Grand Forks in 1961. Besides training visually-handicapped young people at the school, it now also gives guidance and instructional help to visually-impaired students across the state.

187—The first building at the University of North Dakota, Grand Forks

190—First college building at Mayville

188—Old Main, North Dakota Agricultural College (NDSU), Fargo

191—Minot Normal School

189—Fargo College

192—Building first used for Dickinson Normal School classes

193—State School for the Deaf, Devils Lake, built in 1892

The first state teacher-training institutions opened at Mayville and Valley City in 1890. Since the legislature did not provide money for them, private donations supported the two schools their first two years. The first summer school for teachers opened in 1902 at Valley City. As grade schools began to hold terms through fall, winter, and spring, more and more teachers began attending summer school in order to earn certificates.

At Valley City, instruction began in a rented room in the public school with a Congregational minister as teacher and principal. Two years later the school moved into its first building (now McFarland Hall). In 1987, Valley City State College became Valley City State University.

The second state legislature provided funds for Mayville Normal School's first building. Now known as "Old Main," it was constructed in 1893. In 1925 the school became a four- year college, and in 1987 it was approved as Mayville State University.

When the University of North Dakota faculty at Grand Forks examined their first thirteen students in September, 1884, not one student was found qualified for college studies. Some students were not ready for high school. So the university president, W. M. Blackburn, taught reading and American history instead of the college courses he had planned to teach. Three other teachers on the staff also taught high school courses until students were ready for college work.

University teachers and students lived and studied in the Main Building. They hauled drinking water out from Grand Forks. The fringe of settlement was then only seventy miles to the west.

After the depression of 1893, the state legislature provided so little money for the University that it appeared the school must close. Grand Forks citizens then raised funds for paying the teachers and to keep the school operating until the state again provided support.

The North Dakota Agricultural College admitted its first six students on September 8, 1891. The first classes met in rented quarters until faculty and students could move out to Main Building. Fields surrounded it on every side, and with the new state experiment station close by, this land-grant college offered tuition-free training to state residents. It became North Dakota State University in 1960.

The first school of its kind in the United States, the State Manual Training school was established at Ellendale in 1899 and later added teacher-training courses, becoming Ellendale Normal School, and later a four-year college. It next became the Ellendale Branch of the University of North Dakota. Dwindling enrollments, a disastrous fire that destroyed two buildings, and competition from other schools for appropriations brought its closing in 1970. Two years later, by a referendum vote, North Dakotans sold the entire campus for one dollar to Trinity Bible Institute of Jamestown. It is now Trinity Bible College.

NDSU-Bottineau first opened as the State School of Forestry in 1907 in temporary quarters. Teacher training courses were added in 1918, and the school became a junior college in 1925. In 1969 the school became affiliated with the North Dakota State University, Fargo. as NDSU-Bottineau and Institute of Forestry.

As the western part of the state became settled, the need arose for another normal school. One opened at Minot in 1913. Eleven faculty members welcomed fifty students to class in the city armory until the first campus building was built. Because the school could not afford enough chairs for all classrooms, each student carried his chair with him from class to class. The school is now Minot State University.

Another normal school opened at Dickinson five years later with a two-year program for training elementary and secondary teachers. In 1931, it became a four-year teachers college and in 1987 it became Dickinson State University.

Bismarck State College was a Depression-era experiment. Originally known as Bismarck Junior College, it was created in 1939 in response to a community need for a local college. It held its first classes in the Bismarck High School. Its present campus is located on the northwest edge of Bismarck.

In 1941 the Devils Lake Junior College and Business School began operation as part of the Devils Lake public school system. During the Sixties, it added technical and vocational programs, and enrollments steadily increased. After acquiring its own campus, it moved into its first building complex in 1966. Twenty-one years later it was renamed University of North Dakota-Lake Region and came under the supervision of the University at Grand Forks.

The University of Mary (Roman Catholic) first opened as a junior college in 1955. Its main campus is seven miles south of Bismarck, overlooking the Missouri River.

In the fall of 1957, the University of North Dakota began offering extension classes at Williston. Enrollments grew so that the UND-Williston was founded in 1961 with classes held in local school buildings. In 1967 it moved into its first facility on its present 80-acre campus.

In 1910 about 30 percent of farm boys finished sixth grade and less than one percent completed high school. Half of the teachers who taught in rural schools had never taught before—and this continued into the 1930s. Half of North Dakota youngsters attended one-room schools during the state's first half century.

Peak number of one-room rural schools was reached in 1927-1928 with a total of 4,750 such schools. As the rural areas lost population during the hard times of the Twenties and the drouth and depression of the Thirties, many rural schools closed. During the Fifties, school districts began consolidating into larger units, and a few counties became a single school district. As a result, more one-room schools closed as farm pupils took buses to schools in town. By the Sixties, the number of one-room schools had dropped to less than five hundred. Only eleven one-room schools were operating in 1990.

Because of the sparse population, particularly in the western part of the state, many farm children lived too far from a high school to attend. To help such youngsters continue their education beyond eighth grade, T. W. Thordarson, an instructor at North Dakota Agricultural College, outlined a plan by which rural young people could study high school subjects by correspondence. He presented his idea to the Farmers Union which in turn introduced a bill to the legislature which in 1934 implemented the State Division of Supervised Study now located at NDSU, Fargo.

As with the one-room rural schools, a large number of small high schools began closing as motor buses made possible larger consolidated school areas. From a peak number of 630 high schools during the Twenties, the number has decreased to 235, most of which are accredited.

Public school enrollment reached an all-time high of 176,382 in 1923. As state population declined, school enrollment continued to drop. In 1989, there were 126,435 students enrolled in all the elementary and secondary schools in the state.

194—Dirt farmer and son

9 - Dirt Farming

A "dirt farmer" will have you know that he is the man who tills his own soil. He is not the banker or the merchant who owns a farm and hires other men to do the work.

The young dirt farmer of today takes for granted the standard shipping rate. But pioneer Dakota farmers paid whatever the railway charged them. Big businesses not only obtained lower shipping rates than farmers, but they were also given rebates. Railway rates varied according to locality, and they were high in North Dakota.

Farmers paid more for a short haul than big business paid for a long haul. In the 1870s, freight on a car of salt from Chicago to Saint Paul was $35. But when that same car of salt was sent on to Willmar, Minnesota (one-fourth the distance) freight charges were $73. In those years, Red River Valley farmers paid 30 cents a bushel on grain shipped from Moorhead to Duluth.

During North Dakota's first quarter century, the farmer brought his grain to an elevator owned by the railway or by an association of grain-buyers headquartering in Duluth or Minneapolis. Railways refused to provide cars to farmers.

At such elevators, the farmer was cheated by grain grading. Wheat which appeared to the farmer as of No. 1 quality, many elevator men graded as No. 3 or No. 4. At Minneapolis, and other large grain

195—Statue of John Burke in National Hall of Fame in the Rotunda of the U. S. Capitol

shipping points, different grades of wheat were mixed before selling to millers who would grind it into flour. Grain bought from the farmer as No. 3 or 4 was sold by the grain trader to the miller as No. 1 or 2.

The local elevator docked the farmer for screenings (grain not good enough to be used), yet the farmer paid the freight on the screenings to Minneapolis. And in Minneapolis, wheat which the farmer had been told was "not fit for the hogs" was ground into flour for people. The farmer had to accept whatever price the Minneapolis grain monopoly set on his produce.

The North Dakota Bankers Association in 1906 sent a committee to Duluth and Minneapolis to investigate. The committee found that while one large Minnesota storage elevator, in a three months' period, purchased 99,711 bushels of No. 1 Northern wheat—it shipped out 196,288 bushels of the same grade. They found other examples of how the North Dakota farmer was swindled.

When a farmer sold his wheat to a flour mill at Minot, he paid freight charges on the wheat to Minneapolis though the wheat was not shipped there, but was ground into flour at Minot. When this farmer went to the grocery store to buy a sack of Minot-made flour, he also paid freight on that flour from Minneapolis!

The dirt farmer also learned that when he got a bank loan he had to pay higher interest than his storekeeper friend did. While such unfairness became known, the farmer had no way to stop it.

Because a large number of North Dakota farmers had been born in Europe, many could not understand or read English. So they had trouble even swapping livestock or doing business with a neighbor. Still more difficult for them was to try to understand the marketing system. The immigrant farmer learned to fear or distrust what he could not understand. But as immigrant and American-born farmers helped one another, they realized they must join together in order to better their cause. After all, did not farmers make up three-fourths of the state population?

But they would learn that it took more than just joining together to bring results in the market place. Farmer movement would follow farmer movement. While farmers agreed they should join together in order to get what they needed, they too much disagreed as to how they could get what they needed.

First there was the Granger movement which brought no improvements except to show farmers they needed political action to get results. There next followed the Alliance which in 1890 had 40,000 farmer members when the total state population was 191,000. But disagreements brought an end to the Alliance movement. This was followed by a political organization, the Populists.

The Populists, joining with the Democrats, elected the "Farmers' Choice" candidate, Eli C. Shortridge, as governor. During the Shortridge administration, the legislature provided for public scales, required trains to run daily, and passed a measure to establish a North Dakota-owned terminal elevator in Minneapolis. (This was never accomplished.)

But the depression of 1893 brought an end to the Populist movement. Then in the 1906 election, "Honest John" Burke was elected as governor. He had seen the injustices done to the common man by banking, milling, and railroad interests. During his administration the legislature established a twine plant at the penitentiary to help farmers get twine at less cost. Railways were required to deliver cars to farmers who wanted to ship grain. During his three terms in office, he succeeded in ridding North Dakota of the notorious political boss, Alexander McKenzie.

Another farmer movement, the American Society of Equity, organized for the purpose of holding grain off the market until it reached a dollar a bushel. The venture failed.

In the election of 1912, the people had approved by a majority of 3 to 1 the establishment of a state-owned elevator. But the legislature opposed this and recommended that no such elevator be built.

Farmers became furious. A group of Equity members in 1915 went to Bismarck to protest to the legislature. They were told not to try to make recommendations to lawmakers but they should "go home and slop the hogs."

Farmers then took "Go home and slop the hogs" as their rallying cry, and a new political party, the Nonpartisan League, was born. It was led by a former Socialist member of the Minnesota legislature, Arthur C. Townley.

Townley started out in a Model T Ford to organize farmers. As the organization grew, other farmers went out to get farmers to join and pay dues. Membership grew. In 1916, 3000 delegates of the 40,000 members of the Nonpartisan League chose candidates for the election. These candidates were of Republican background. That fall all League candidates except one Democrat were elected. In the next election, 1918, the League obtained majority in the legislature.

Again, efforts were made to establish a terminal elevator, this time in North Dakota. Several League measures passed. But again, this movement by farmers lost its power. During World War I people had witnessed the overthrow of the Russian czar by a small Bolshevik minority. They looked with suspicion on Townley's Socialist background. Scandals came from the mishandling of Nonpartisan money. Gradually, farmers turned to the Republican and Democratic parties for political solutions to their problems.

The Farmers Union now gained the attention of dirt farmers. Farmers Union believed in cooperative buying and selling for its members. When they held their first state convention at Jamestown in 1927, more than 13,000 members attended. In North Dakota today, the Farmers Union Oil Cooperative is the second largest distributor of petroleum. Membership in the Farmers Union now totals 29,000 farm families.

The North Dakota Farm Bureau organized at Fargo in 1942. It does not endorse any political

197—Horse gang plow, 1905

198—Harvesting with a binder and early tractor, 1920s

196—Farmstead with harvest field of grain shocks, 1920s (W. P. Sebens photo)

199—Steam threshing rig near Page

200—During the "Dust Bowl" years of the Thirties, wind blew top soil into drifts, 1936.

201—Calves seek forage in a cornfield devastated by grasshoppers, 1936

202—In western North Dakota, 1934, a boy plays by himself near an abandoned plow. Russian thistles grew where nothing else did.

party or political candidate. Farm Bureau people work for the right of the individual to operate with minimum government interference. They believe that as the individual has opportunity to grow strong, so has his nation. Membership in 1990 was nearly 25 thousand, about half of these being farmers and ranchers. The Farm Bureau's Nodak Mutual Insurance Company enrolls subscribers among both rural and urban people.

The Twenties saw the change-over from the use of horse power to tractor power and the promise that a man could handle more work by himself. However, the hard times of the early Twenties were just a foretaste of the troubles farmers would experience during the Thirsty Thirties. Right after the 1929 market crash came the drouth of the 1930s, bringing in ten years of little or no crops, years of dust storms, grasshoppers, cutworms. One year farmers in western North Dakota stacked green Russian thistle to feed the remnants of their cattle herds.

"Don't faint when you read these prices!" wrote Tom Nelson on the market blackboard of the Sanish Farmers Union Elevator when wheat dropped to 50 cents a bushel in 1930. But two years later the price for top-grade wheat there had sunk to 17 cents.

Relief shipments of food and clothing came into the stricken area from Farmers Union members in other states, and from the Red Cross and Federal Government. In 1933, the average personal income in the United States was $375 a year; North Dakotans averaged $145.

Low prices and continuing dry years increased the debts of farmers. Because of the drouth, only 34 percent of the acreage planted to wheat in North Dakota was harvested in 1936. From 1930 to 1944 about a third of farm families lost their farms by foreclosure. Trying to find a livelihood elsewhere, thousands of North Dakotans sought work in Minnesota, Washington, and California.

In Iowa, the Farm Holiday Association organized and spread through the Midwest. The purpose of the Association was to keep farm produce off the market until prices improved.

North Dakota farmers dumped cream into hog troughs instead of selling it for 17 cents a pound. Because farmers had no income to pay off their debts, hundreds of farms were subject to foreclosure. Angry farmer friends gathered at foreclosure sales. They bid 2 or 3 cents for a cow or horse or tractor, a penny for a man's cookstove—and saw to it that no bids went higher. Then, the sale over, they returned the goods to the farmer on permanent loan.

Governor William Langer proclaimed a moratorium on farm evictions because of debts and this was later upheld by the North Dakota legislature. A year later, Congress passed the Frazier-Lemke Act which gave farmers five years in which to pay their debts.

Eastern newspaper reporters visited North Dakota during the drouth and wrote that North Dakota was becoming a barren desert. Bismarck residents rode bicycles across the dry bed of the Missouri. Cattle died on the western prairies, starved to death where even the Russian Thistles one year did not grow.

But the dry cycle passed. Rain and good crops again blessed the state. Crops during World War II were the largest ever produced in the state. Thousands of people, though, left the state to work in defense plants. With far fewer farm workers, farmers put in longer hours and bought more tractors and power equipment.

Rural electrification came to lighten work loads on the farm. First line went into operation at Cando in 1937. Today a farm without electricity is unusual.

When North Dakota entered the Union, the average farmer tilled 277 acres. The largest number of farms in North Dakota was reached in 1935 with a total of 77,975 with farms averaging slightly over 462 acres. By 1989, there were 33,500 farms. The average size of the farm had increased to 1,209 acres.

North Dakota continues as the most agricultural state in the Union, but most North Dakotans no longer live on farms and in rural villages. This change came about in 1990 when population figures showed slightly more people residing in cities and towns than in the rural areas.

The bonanza wheat farms of the Red River Valley knew a short and spectacular life. So did the open-range ranches of western North Dakota. Following the homesteading period, agricultural land was farmed in family-sized units which raised both grain and livestock. In the Twenties and early Thirties about 40,000 seasonal laborers found work on North Dakota farms. With mechanized equipment taking the place of horse power, the number of seasonal workers on farms has been reduced to an estimated 6 to 7 thousand. And today jobs in town and other off-farm work account for nearly half of the average farm family's earnings.

10 - The Taming of Big Muddy

The Missouri River in North Dakota no longer rampages in flood-stage binges, uprooting trees, digging new channels, stealing acres from fields and pastures, and carrying away tons of good soil.

Seventy miles upstream from Bismarck, one of the world's largest rolled-earth dams has harnessed the Missouri, converting its surge of power into enough electricity for a city of a million people. This

203—This drawing by Edward A. Dunlavy shows how the Garrison Dam's main structure is 7 feet 6 inches taller than the 19-story state capitol.

Garrison Dam forms a reservoir larger than either Lake Huron or Lake Ontario. The amount of water held back by the bouldered embankments of the dam is as much water as flows past Sioux City, Iowa, in one year. In its two-mile length, the dam contains 70 million yards of dirt, enough to fill a freight train reaching half way around the globe.

Drive along the highway rimming the top of the dam and you will see its 249-foot high intake structure. However, you see only the part which rises above the water. You will find it difficult to believe that this intake structure is actually seven feet taller than the skyscraper capitol in Bismarck. In this $200 million dam, enough concrete was used to build a standard highway from Bismarck to Chicago.

Of the eight tunnels in the dam, three are for flood control, and five for power. The five are 29 feet in diameter, the others smaller—but still big enough so that a train or truck could run through. When filled to capacity, the reservoir reaches upriver 200 miles and has a 1,340-mile shoreline.

Construction began in 1947 with the building of a town, Riverdale, where the men who would work on the dam could live. Also a steel construction bridge was built across the stream. First big project on the actual dam was to dig a channel through which water could flow out of the main stream bed.

Fleets of earth-moving machines swarmed over the Missouri bottom lands. Power shovels each took bites of earth big enough to fill an average kitchen. The shovels dumped these bites into trucks so big their tires could be changed only by derricks. Men

204—Aerial view of Garrison Dam (looking west)

worked under floodlights at night, and they worked when the temperature hit 110 degrees in the shade or dropped below zero. The dam was completed in July, 1950.

Not all men rejoiced over the big dam. For some it brought heartache. It took from them homes they loved. Farmers, ranchers, and Fort Berthold Reservation Indians knew their best lands would be flooded. While the Government paid them for the lands they lost, the payment was seldom equal to the value placed on it by the owner. And there were losses that could not be compensated by money.

Many who lost their homes had to change their way of life and find different work. Some believed the cost of the dam was higher than it should be. They insisted that small dams on smaller streams would help more in flood control. Not all land, they said, can be irrigated.

To escape the rising waters of the reservoir, people in Sanish and Van Hook built New Town. On Fort Berthold Indian Reservation, the Indian headquarters town of Elbowoods had to be evacuated. Some folks remarked that even the rattlesnakes had to crawl out of their river dens to seek their own Mount Ararat.

The flooding waters brought the hardest adjustments to the people of the Fort Berthold Indian Reservation. For generations these people had lived along Grandmother River, and she had been more than just a stream of water to them. Grandmother River had been the Place of Home. Now 155,000 acres of the richest bottom lands where 90 percent of the Indians had lived and farmed were taken from them. The deep waters of the reservoir would separate the remaining 480,000 acres of the Reservation into five parts of high plateaus, canyons and buttes. Such land could hardly provide farming or ranching for 2,000 Indian people.

About 300 of them chose to leave the Reservation, seeking employment in cities. While many adjusted quickly to the change, others found it difficult. Some bitterly denounced the Crooked-Tongued who broke treaties at their own convenience.

Before the waters began to rise, archeologists hurried to the sites of Fort Berthold and of Like-a-Fishhook Village to dig for artifacts. All buildings were put on wheels and hauled up the hills to new locations. The Four Bears Bridge across the Missouri at Elbowoods was taken apart and used as the center span of a new 4,482-foot long bridge across the reservoir just south of where the Verendrye Bridge and Sanish had been. About 2,000 bodies were moved from the military cemetery for soldiers and Indian scouts and from the Indian burial grounds.

One of the last buildings to leave Elbowoods was Memorial Church. It had been named in honor of the Congregational missionary, the Reverend C. L. Hall. He had come to Fort Berthold in 1876 and built his House of Eyes and worked among the Indians with his Book. All the way up the hills as the building was moved, the steeple bell clanged, sounding to the Indians who heard it, as a protest against leaving the beloved valley.

In North Dakota, lesser dams added to the conservation of water. Dickinson Dam provides water for irrigation and aids flood control on the Heart River. So does the Heart Butte Dam south of Glen Ullin. Jamestown Dam on the James River helps control floods and supplies the city of Jamestown with water. The Baldhill Dam on the Sheyenne does the same for Valley City. Homme Dam on Park River provides the city of Park River with water.

In 1967, Senator Quentin Burdick of North Dakota introduced a bill in Congress for re-naming the Garrison Dam Reservoir. President Lyndon Johnson signed this bill into law, making the reservoir's official name Lake Sakakawea.

Back in 1904, a University of North Dakota professor had been hired by a citizens' group to explore the possibilities of getting water from the Missouri for irrigation. He gave them his considered opinion: it would be impossible to tame the Big Muddy with a dam.

11 - From under the Good Earth

Sixty percent of the lignite coal deposits of the United States lies under 32,000 North Dakota acres. North Dakota has 19 percent of all solid fuel reserves in the nation, and the discovery of "black liquid gold" placed it among leading states in oil production.

Where twenty years earlier the parched earth had grown little else than Russian Thistle, the first oil derricks thrust into the big sky of the prairie. Plus this, North Dakota has deposits of minerals in quantities little realized by the average resident of the state.

Lewis and Clark found lignite outcroppings in the Knife River area and they used it for blacksmithing at Fort Mandan. A few river steamers occasionally burned this "brown coal" that had dried in the sun. Military and trading posts away from timbered areas used lignite coal. Early cowpunchers discovered underground fires feeding on lignite veins in the Badlands.

Homesteaders in western North Dakota began to pick away at the 600 billion tons in the state. Harvest done, they stacked lignite coal chunks in large piles near their houses.

When Jim Johnson in April of 1883 had staked his claim on the Souris River, he built a campfire. The next morning, though all the wood had been consumed, the fire still burned because it had ignited a layer of coal underneath.

That fall, after building his shack, Johnson dug out six tons from the first mine in the Burlington area. Later, his father-in-law, J. L. Coltan, also opened a mine on his claim, and he took out 20 tons. As railways extended into the territory, coal was shipped out. One of the first to ship out was the Mouse River Lignite Coal Company near Burlington. It took out a hundred tons daily during its first years.

Coal mining companies now developed in widespread places. Strip-mining began in 1919, first with the use of horse-drawn scrapers and elevating graders, then with power equipment.

About 290 million dollars' worth of lignite is mined annually in North Dakota. This is mined from a source that can supply the entire United States with fuel energy for generations to come. From a lump of lignite coal can be produced heat or power, and some thirty by-products including such different human needs as tar, stain, paint, wax, water softener, oil, disinfectant, soap, perfume, wood preservative, gasoline, and plastics.

It took longer to find the black liquid treasure. As early as 1900, Ward County residents insisted that

205—An A. C. Townley oil rig

oil would some day be found in the Souris River valley because several farmers complained that oil in certain springs made the water unfit to drink.

Seven years later a dry gas erupted from a water well drilled in Bottineau County. While the supply lasted, the towns of Westhope and Landa piped it in for lighting. By 1909, a total of 25 gas wells had been drilled in Bottineau, LaMoure, and Williams Counties.

Some folks kept insisting there must be oil under the sod. So drilling for oil was done at Lone Tree, Glenfield, and Robinson with no results. A. C. Townley, the Nonpartisan League leader, organized a company which drilled the "Big Viking" in Williams County in 1917. No oil. During the next thirty years, fifteen more drillings resulted in dry holes. Over twenty years later, the Big Viking derrick was still standing when the California Company drilled in the same section of land and gave up at 10,281 feet.

In the 1890s, John Iverson brought his family from Norway and homesteaded near what is now Tioga. John's son, Clarence, noticed an oily substance on the water which the cattle drank. He kept telling his father that there must be oil under their farm. Clarence watched the drilling of Big Viking and the California well and though neither produced oil, he continued to believe there was oil.

Then in the fall of 1950, Amerado Petroleum Corporation moved its drilling rig into a field from which Clarence Iverson had just harvested wheat. That winter a small show of oil came, and on April 4, 1951, the crude oil gushed up. Suddenly, Tioga, a village of 450 people, overflowed with lease hunters. A second well brought oil in June, a third in October, and a fourth in November. On October 24th, Governor Norman Brunsdale dedicated a granite oil discovery monument on Clarence Iverson's farm. Though the weather was nasty, 4000 happy North Dakotans atttended the ceremony.

The oil fever spread as outsiders swarmed into hotels at Minot, Williston, and Bismarck. A brisk business started in the buying of leases from farmers and other landowners.

Oil workers and their families crowded every possible living space in Tioga and overflowed into neighboring Williston. Oil workers' children squeezed into classrooms once large enough for village and farm pupils. Contractors built houses with all haste and shipped in pre-fabricated dwellings. Tioga which in 1951 had ranked 117th in size in the state grew rapidly until it became the fourteenth largest city in the state.

In the 18 months following the discovery on Iverson's farm, 224 producing wells and 41 dry holes were completed in what is known as the Nesson Anticline. And North Dakotans, seeing a new industry bringing new income into the state, planned for pipe lines and refineries. They learned to talk about swabbing, dual recovery, mineral acres, cat crackers, stinkers, pebble pups, roughnecks, spudding, pay zones, and monkey belts.

In the year of discovery, the total crude oil production amounted to 26,724 barrels. Peak oil production was reached in 1984 with a total of 52.6 million barrels of oil.

North Dakota farmers, however, even with the odor of sludge pools in their nostrils, proudly observe that wheat is still king and that agriculture brings in 63 percent of the state's gross income.

Other minerals also lie under the good earth. Vast deposits of rock salt are buried beneath the northwestern prairies of the state. This salt can be used for snow and ice removal, stock feed, food preservation, and water softening.

It is estimated that 500 billion tons of potash could be recovered in the state. Potash serves chiefly as a soil fertilizer.

Both rock salt and potash are mined by injecting water down into the bed and then pumping the mineral out. A salt-mining plant operated in the Williston area for several years.

In various parts of the state we find clays of different kinds. Some local potters have used such clays. Other kinds of clay are made into face brick, building tile, and fire brick.

One of North Dakota's oldest manufacturing concerns is the Hebron Brick Company which has operated since 1904. After a large clay deposit was discovered six miles north of Hebron, Charles Weigeland and Ferdinand Leutz began the brick factory. Present production is 20 million bricks each year.

Other minerals of value include sand and gravel deposits, uranium in Billings County, scoria in western counties used for road surfacing, stone for crushing and riprapping dams and stream channels, sandstone that has been used in buildings.

12 - The Peace Garden State

Many men who once lived along their beloved Grandmother River lie buried an ocean away in Flanders Field. North Dakota Indian warriors fought well in World War I. When the second World War began, more Indians volunteered—in proportion to their number—than any other race in the United States.

About 31,000 Native Americans now live in the Peace Garden State. Ten thousand of these live off Reservations, chiefly in the cities of Bismarck, Grand Forks, Minot, and Williston. The Chippewas of the Turtle Mountain Indian Reservation presently form the largest Indian population, numbering 9,800. At Fort Berthold Indian Reservation, the Three Affiliated Tribes total 3,310. There are 3,580 Sioux at the Fort Totten Indian Reservation, and 4,017 in the North Dakota area of the Standing Rock Indian Reservation.

Recent years have seen the establishment of an accredited tribal community college at each of the Reservations as well as the development of special industries.

In its beginning, North Dakota had more foreign-born residents than any other state. While Americans had come to settle Dakota first, their number was soon eclipsed by northern Europeans eager to homestead the free and fertile land available to them. When the railway crossed the Red River in 1872, only about 2,500 whites lived in northern Dakota. When North Dakota became a state, the population was climbing to 191,000. By 1910, the number of immigrants settled in the state were 125,000 Norwegians, 117,000 Germans and German-Russians, 73,000 English, 29,000 Swedes, and 13,000 Danes.

The eastern valley region is peopled mostly by those of Norwegian ancestry. The central portion contains a mixture of Germans, Scandinavians, and German Russians. The northern part is Norwegian with areas of English Canadians.

Though the state has long had the reputation of being Scandinavian, the largest group of immigrants spoke German. Norway did provide more North Dakotans than any other European nation, but the second largest immigrant group came from Russia, and about 90 percent of these spoke German. This was because they had at one time migrated to Ukrainian Russia from Germany. Add to them the large number of settlers coming directly from Germany, and the result is more North Dakotans of German-speaking ancestry than of Norwegian.

Church membership in the state reflects the religious persuasions of the immigrants. The Lutheran Church, followed by the Roman Catholic, holds largest membership. In 1906 about 70 percent of the churches used foreign languages. By the Twenties and Thirties such use had largely been discontinued.

A great influx of settlers flowed into the state until 1920. Then in the Thirties and Forties, North Dakota saw many people leaving the state. The state's peak population of 680,845 occurred in 1930. The most recent count puts the number of North Dakotans at 650,000.

The Great Depression beginning in 1929 reduced employment and property values. A second disaster soon struck in North Dakota with the devastating drouth of the Thirties and the destruction by crop pests. For two years the pasture lands did not even green in parts of western North Dakota, and only Russian Thistle survived the scorching winds and driving dust storms. Grasshoppers and cut worms ruined what crops did grow.

A third calamity struck the state on December 29, 1930, when the state capitol burned in three hours to a shell of charred walls. Governor George Schafer arrived from St. Paul at the height of the blaze. With not enough water and hose, the fire could not be controlled.

Secretary of State Robert Byrne broke through a window in his office to save the original copy of the state constitution. Frank Bryant, the Governor's secretary, rescued the portraits of the governors.

Several days later, the ruin cooled enough that workmen could open the vaults. They found documents covering upwards of 70 million dollars' worth of state investments safe in the treasurer's vault. Contents in several other department vaults were also unharmed, but all files and records not in vaults were destroyed.

The first unit of the destroyed building had been erected in 1885 at a cost of $100,000. In 1894 a south wing had been added, costing $50,000; and ten years later, the north wing cost twice that amount.

Until a new capitol could be built, state government offices were housed in different Bismarck buildings, including the entire second floor of the Patterson Hotel. The legislature held its sessions in the Burleigh County Memorial Building.

Only a hundred persons gathered to lay the granite boulder cornerstone of the new capitol on September 5, 1933. This was the fiftieth anniversary of the Dakota Territorial Capitol cornerstone-laying which had been attended by hundreds of

206—A farm woman burns dried corn cobs in her cook stove during the Depression

207—Rags are stuffed around a kitchen window to keep out the dust

208—A small village store goes out of business, 1928

98¢ Jacket

Yes sir, it's really true. A good warm "chore coat" of good quality full 2:20 weight demin, triple stitched, three large pockets and safty watch pocket. Fancy plaid blanket lining makes this coat ideal for wearing in the cold days of fall and winter.
Mens sizes 36 to 46

1.00

SOLD FOR EVERYDAY WEAR ONLY

A wonderful bargain for men who work in shops or in the fields. These hats will wear.

On Mens Work Clothing At Your Johnson Store

For Instance here's a chambray

WORK SHIRT

For **39¢**

A medium weight, dark blue chambray shirt, made in standard size and finish. A cool, comfortable shirt for everyday wear.

All Sizes At All Five Stores

Would You Believe It?
CHILD'S LEATHER

SHOE

Childs Sizes 5 to 11½
Misses Sizes 12 to 2

75¢ Each Pair

No, it's not a misprint, 75¢ is the price; a really and truly leather shoe with black composition sole, all sizes, little tots from size 5 up to the school miss wearing a size 2.

Your Johnson Co. store thru mass buying in original cases direct from the manufacturers and again selling for cash, gives you always a big value for your money.

Black Leather uppers, flexible stitchdown soles of black composition.

12 inch firepot **$21.75**

Mens Dress Shirt

Sizes 14½ to 17

The latest and greatest of our mens bargains in dress wear. A large assortment of snappy patterns, and pleasing colors. Guaranteed absolutely fast colors, and well made thruout.
EVERY SHIRT CELLPHANE WRAPPED.

OVERALLS TOO
39¢ to 98¢

ndid School Hose
Looking, fine comb-
a hose that will
ndid wear.

17

ads of pairs
ood hose
e sold by our
e past year.
t of 66 dozen
ved to replen-
tocks, so
we have
and color

OD COLORS
t black and a pleasing
dark tan (Biscuit) in
to 9. YOU SAVE MON-
ERY AT YOUR JOHNSON
STORE

d BOYS OXFORDS
Mens Oxford

198

s a good looking black
of side leather, genuine
r welt composition sole
zes too, at the same low

s A Fancy Number

in Ladies rayon
clocked black French
Heel stocking. Some-
thing different and
real clever looking.
Comes in shades of
white, tan and
boulevard with Black
French Heel and
black clocking up
the side. They're
real nifty look-
ing and give the
appearance of a
much higher
priced stocking.
Our Cash
Price
Only .79¢

79¢

Fashioned hose for $1.00

NIFTY LEATHER
OXFORDS

98¢

Here's a good looking oxford, and one that will give service Black and Ivory, or Tan and Ivory. Sizes 6 to 2   98¢

Don't Miss This Big Value!
Men's Nainsook Athletic

Union Suits

Ordinarily you can't touch such quality as this for this sale price. But a lucky purchase shoved the price way down and we are passing the saving on to you. Large buttoned flap, closed crotch, strongly sewed. Exactly as pictured.

Sizes 34 to 46

69c

Sport Shirts
49c 69c

Tailored like a man's, of soft yarn in pastels and white. Small, medium and large.

"Swing"
Slacks

Extra wide sweep and colorful stripes.
Sizes 14 to 20

98c

Others at 49c and 79c

Misses White Straps

98c
$1.18

8½ to 2

STRAPS or TIES, they're made for service but neat and stylish in appearance.

YOUNG MEN'S

DRESS PANTS

$1.00 Our regular
$2.95 values

TWEEDS
MIXTURES
GREYS
TANS

YES, they are our regular $2.95 quality dress trousers, young mens styles, 22 inch bottoms, pleated or regular models, belt loops, buckle tabs at side, good pockets, stylish appearing. Soft finished WOOLENS, light spring patterns. THESE WILL

SUBSTANTIAL WORK SHOES
They're Made To Wear

148

This work shoe is made of a first quality full grain (not split) leather, double tanned to withstand moisture. Leather in-sole, outsole of hard wearing, black composition.

Sizes 6½ to 11 priced at $1.48

Other work shoes at $2.38 to $3.35

Beautiful Monarch Range

This shows you our NEW MONARCH with all white enamel finish. Large copper reservoir, patented Mirco top, large oven.

OUR CASH PRICE $125.00

OTHER MONARCHS AS LOW AS 67.50

Sensational Value in Beatiful Apron Dresses

again Your Johnson Store
Takes The Lead In

59

offering you these dainty and cleverly styled dresses at our surprisingly low price. Such an assortment of pretty designs and styles to choose from. These come in the popular new Silhouette in modified princess lines with wide flare skirts.

Some with V necks
Some with collars
Some with Bows
Some with Belts

White background with many pretty assorted floral designs of red, green, lavender, pink, blue and other colors.

You will indeed be delighted with this wonderful bargain that we are offering. We invite you to come into our stores and see for yourself these pretty dresses. We feel confident that you will agree with us that they are all we say they are.

COME EARLY AND SELECT YOUR STYLE

209—"Rock bottom" prices during the hard times of the Twenties and Thirties

pioneers, ex-President U. S. Grant, and dozens of out-of-state officials.

The 19-story skyscraper capitol was completed in 1935 for slightly less than two million dollars. Not all people approved of it. Some called it a "silo on the hill," for it was very different from the usual domed seat of government.

The North Dakota capitol has 80 percent usable space as contrasted with only 29 percent usable space in neighboring Minnesota's state house. Nebraska's capitol, dedicated in 1932 and costing five times that of North Dakota's state house, has 50 percent usable space.

While plans were made for the skyscraper capitol, Americans and Canadians gathered on July 14, 1932, in the Turtle Mountains. Here they dedicated an international garden to the praise of peace. Where the lake-studded and timbered area sprawls like a monstrous turtle above the surrounding prairies, a tract of 2,340 acres has been set aside to memorialize the friendship of two nations.

More than 25,000 persons came to stand about the simple cairn of native stone raised on the international boundary line—an American flag on one side, a Canadian on the other. The cairn plaque has this inscription: "To God in His glory, we two nations dedicate this garden, and pledge ourselves that as long as men shall live, we will not take arms against one another."

In the years since then, Americans and Canadians have donated money and worked as volunteers together. They have built in this International Peace Garden sunken pools, beautiful gardens, peace memorials, an amphitheatre, a carillon bell tower, miniature lakes, a chapel, and living accomodations for the thousands of people who visit. Throughout each summer, artist teachers, famous guest conductors and outstanding clinicians instruct at week-long music camps for talented young musicians.

Thousands visit the Garden each year. The license plates of North Dakota cars and trucks advertise the Garden wherever North Dakotans drive.

For a century, North Dakota has led the nation in spring wheat production. It is the nation's leading grower of durum wheat, supplying 70 percent of U. S. production. It is also first in rye and flax. It supplies 34 percent of the nation's navy beans, 20 percent of pinto beans, 14 percent of dry edible beans, and 10 percent of sugar beets. The Red River Valley, the third largest potato-growing region in America, has long been famous for its dryland potatoes.

A crop unknown to North Dakota farmers of early times is the sunflower; the state now ranks first in growing sunflowers, providing 80 percent of the nation's supply. Another new source of agricultural income is honey. Out-of-state beekeepers

210—The new capitol shortly after it was completed in 1935

211—Aerial view of central portion of International Peace Garden

212—Floral clock at the Peace Garden

213—The geographical center of North America is identified by this stone marker at Rugby.

214—The Danish windmill at Kenmare

bring their hives into the state during summer months because our sunflowers, alfalfa, and sweet clover produce top-quality honey. There are nearly 500 beekeepers and more than thirty commercial apiaries here.

Livestock ranks second to wheat in farm income. Most of this is in beef cattle raised in the western part of the state. There are over 93,000 dairy cows producing over a billion pounds of milk each year. About 350,000 hogs are raised each year, and about 170,000 sheep. Nearly twenty meat-packing plants show that the Marquis de Mores had the right idea.

While North Dakota continues as a leading agricultural state, other industries increase in importance. The Grant-Thorton study of general manufacturing climates in the United States ranks North Dakota as No. 1. Why? We have a work force that outproduces the national average. Most North Dakotans have grown up on a farm "Where you can't call in sick to the cows." On the farm we learned early how to pitch in and get the job done. So we have a work ethic that commands the respect of employers and investors.

Manufacturing has grown greatly in recent decades and now earns 12 percent of the state income. In 1990 there were 85 manufacturers of farm equipment and implements in the state, 48 food processing companies utilizing agricultural produce. Thousands of North Dakota people now find employment in the making of a great variety of things.

In 1989, more than two million tourists relaxed in North Dakota, bringing in an estimated total income of $700 million. Folks at home as well as out-of-state visitors find a variety of recreation here: sailing and fishing on Lake Sakakawea, exploring the rugged beauty of Theodore Roosevelt National Park, absorbing the history and lore of paleface and Indian at historic sites and museums; camping, swimming, hiking, bird-watching in state parks; and "getting away from it all" in national grasslands, state woodlands and nature preserves.

In North Dakota we have the only Omega Station in North America. At LaMoure, the Omega Station tower is operated by the U. S. Coast Guard. It began operation on October 1, 1972, and its navigation signals are used for transportation in all three mediums: land, sea, and air. Other Omega stations are in Argentina, Australia, Hawaii, Japan, Liberia, Norway, and on Le Reunion, an island in the Indian Ocean.

At Rugby, a monument marks the geographical center of North America. At Jamestown we see the world's largest buffalo—a 60-ton concrete mammoth that stands 60 feet high and is 46 feet long. Built in 1902 by Christian C. Jensen, an immigrant, the Danish windmill at Kenmare is the only one of its kind in the United States. The 2,063-foot KTHI television tower near Mayville is the tallest structure on the North American continent.

The only jewel bearing plant in the United States is at Rolla. The tiny bearings are made for the U. S. Government stockpile of strategic materials and for manufacturers to use in aircraft instruments and missile mechanisms. Most of the highly-skilled workers are Chippewa Indians from the nearby Reservation. The plant is owned by the U. S. Government and it has operated under the direction of the Bulova Watch Company since 1953.

North Dakota has the lowest incidence of AIDS in the United States. It is second after Utah for low mortality from nine chronic diseases, has frequently ranked first for low infant mortality. A recent study placed the state second in the nation in sixteen different health-related areas.

North Dakota residents today look out upon a landscape softened by shelterbelts and farmstead plantings where the homesteaders knew a sea of grass—and carried water to nourish their tree seedlings.

Credit for past accomplishments is too often given to a small number of persons who worked in the right place at the right time. But just as unnamed trappers and hunters went before the earliest named explorers, so it is the unremembered men and women on farms and in prairie towns who built North Dakota, who made it possible for a few to serve as remembered leaders.

The fur seekers and the gold dust searchers came to get what they could for themselves, and they are no more. Those who came to stay and to build sprang from generations work- hardened in toil as fishermen and as farmers in northern Europe. America-fevered they were, and they came to this unsheltered land eager for free land, for homes for themselves, their children and their children's children. The prairie was no place for the timid, the weak, the insincere. They did not turn back, these Scandinavians, Germans, German-Russians, and Canadians. They forgot their ethnic differences in the unity of American citizenship and purpose.

Their sodhuts huddled in blizzards, and their tarpaperd shanties shuddered in thunderstorms, but these folks persevered. They built better dwellings and litle white schoolhouses and spired churches. Where no water flowed, their scrawny windmills nosed into the wind and pumped. This people struggled with drouth, grasshoppers, dust storms, wheat rust and blight, the long miles from a doctor; and those who did not give up earned for their children and children's children a better life than they had known.

A man stands tall in the prairie sun. He has elbow room. He breathes un-smogged air. He lives where the sky arches big. As the world grows smaller about him, he recognizes that he is privileged with a quality of life unknown to most of his fellowmen.

His state provides much food to the world, and energy for the nation. He lives among friendly and industrious people, and he knows that it is people who are North Dakota's greatest asset.

NORTH DAKOTA CHRONOLOGY

1610 Hudson Bay watershed claimed by England because of Henry Hudson's explorations. This included land drained by the Souris and Red Rivers.

1670 Souris and Red River area became part of the Hudson's Bay Company domain.

1682 LaSalle, French explorer, claimed Missouri watershed for France.

1738 First recorded exploration by white men in North Dakota area. Pierre de la Verendrye, searching for a way to the Pacific Ocean, also claimed explored area for France.

1742-43 Verendrye's sons continued explorations.

1760 English captured Montreal. French fur posts in western territory were abandoned.

1762 France transferred land claimed by LaSalle to Spain.

1763 Following her defeat in the French and Indian War, France gave up all claims to possessions in North America.

1792 D'Eglise, first white man to ascend Missouri River, reached Mandan Indians.

1797 David Thompson, English geographer, explored and mapped northern part of state. Chaboillez opened trading post at Pembina.

1800 Alexander Henry the Younger had fur trade post at Park River.

1801 By secret treaty, Spain returned Mississippi-Missouri territory to France. Henry the Younger moved fur trading post to Pembina.

1802 First nonf-Indian child (Black) born in North Dakota area (at Pembina).

1803 Louisiana Purchase made southwestern part of state United States territory.

1804-05 Lewis and Clark built Fort Mandan and wintered there.

1807 First white child born (Pembina). Fur trader Manuel Lisa came up Missouri in a keelboat.

1808 Missouri Fur Company organized at St. Louis with Lisa as head. John Jacob Astor organized American Fur Company.

1809 Missouri Fur Company established Fort Lisa. Chief Big White returned to the Mandan people.

1811 Northeastern part of state became part of Lord Selkirk's Assiniboia. Bradbury and Nuttal, English botanists, and Brackenridge, American lawyer, visited upper Missouri area.

1812 First Selkirk settlers reached Pembina.

1818 First church and school (Roman Catholic) opened (at Pembina). Northern part of state officially acquired from England though it had been considered U. S. territory previously.

1819 First Yellowstone Expedition failed.

1822 Fort Tilton fur post established.

1823 Stephen H. Long surveyed boundary line at Pembina.

1825 Second Yellowstone Expedition succeeded. Leavenworth Expedition conducted against Arikara Indians.

1826 Kipp's fur post established.

1828 Fort Union opened by American Fur Company.

1831 Fort Clark built by American Fur Company.

1832 **Yellowstone**, first steamer to navigate upper Missouri, reached Fort Union. George Catlin visited Indians of Missouri area.

1833 Prince Maximilian conducted his scientific expedition through upper Missouri. The artist, Karl Bodmer, accompanied him.

1837 Smallpox epidemic devastated upper Missouri Indians, nearly exterminating the Mandans.

1839 Nicollet-Fremont exploration of central area of state.

1842 Rolette opened American Fur Company post at Pembina.

1843 Audubon studied bird and animal life of upper Missouri area. First Red River Cartway begun by Rolette (Pembina to St. Paul).

1845 Fort Berthold fur post opened.

1848 Father Belcourt re-opened mission at Pembina. Barnard and Tanner opened Protestant mission at St. Joseph (now Walhalla). Barnard brought first printing press and melodeon into the state.

1849 Woods Expedition explored Red River Valley. First post office opened (Pembina) with Norman Kittson as postmaster.

1851 Father Belcourt built first flour mill in state (St. Joseph).

1853 Stevens Survey for railway route to Pacific.

1857 Fort Abercrombie, first military post, built.

1859 Charles Bottineau started first farm in state near presentday Walhalla. **Anson Northrop**, first steamer on Red River.

1860 Fort Benton, Montana, became head of Missouri navigation.

1861 Dakota Territory created.

1862 First Territorial legislature met at Yankton. Gold discovered in Montana. Captain James Fisk took his first party of goldseekers across the state. Fort Abercrombie besieged during Sioux Uprising. Little Crow and some followers fled to Devils Lake area.

1863 Dakota Territory opened for homesteading. Sibley and Sully Expeditions conducted against Sioux.

1864 Sully's Second Expedition against the Sioux. Fort Rice built by Sully detachment. Fisk's emigrant party besieged by Indians at Fort Dilts. **Frontier Scout** published at Fort Union.

1866 Fort Buford, military post, established.

1867 Forts Ransom, Totten, and Stevenson built. Treaty with Sisseton and Wahpeton Sioux obtained rights to build railway across Indian lands.

1868 Sioux, influenced by Father De Smet, joined in peace council at Fort Rice. Laramie Treaty defined Great Sioux Reservation. Rolette made first North Dakota homestead entry.

1870 Fort Berthold Indian Reservation boundaries defined. Military post established at Pembina. Treaty made between Chippewas, Sioux, and whites in Red River Valley.

1871 Telegraph line built between Fort Abercrombie and Fort Garry (Winnipeg). Whistler railway survey made west of Missouri.

1872 Stanley railway survey made west of Missouri. Fort Seward replaced Fort Ransom. Fort McKeen built on Missouri. Northern Pacific railway crossed Red River into North Dakota area. First public schools started.

1873 Fort Abraham Lincoln built below Fort McKeen. First issue of Bismarck **Tribune**, state's oldest newspaper, published. Third NP survey made west of Missouri.

1874 Custer Expedition reported gold in the Black Hills.

1875 Bonanza wheat farming started in Red River Valley.

1876 Custer's command annihilated by Sioux at Little Bighorn. First public frame schoolhouse built (Pembina).

1878 Fort Yates built to take the place of Fort Rice.

1879 Open-range bonanza ranching began in Little Missouri country.

1880 Great Northern train crossed Red River into state.

1881 Northern Pacific completed rail construction across the state. Turtle Mountain Indian Reservation established for the Chippewas. First telephone switchboard in state began operation.

1883 Territorial capital moved from Yankton to Bismarck. Marquis de Mores built packing plant and established town of Medora. Teddy Roosevelt started ranching in Medora territory. Final buffalo hunt in the state.

1884 Classes begun at University of North Dakota, Grand Forks.

1885 "Hospital for insane" opened at Jamestown, penitentiary at Bismarck.

1886 Jamestown College opened. "Plenty Snow Winter" ended open-range ranching.

1887 Treaty with Sioux allowed white settlement in Standing Rock area.

1889 North Dakota became a state, with John Miller as first governor. First legislature met at Bismarck.

1890 Normal schools opened at Valley City and Mayville, the agricultural college at Fargo, school for the deaf at Devils Lake, Soldiers' Home at Lisbon. Ghost Dance cult spread among Sioux Indians. Sitting Bull killed. Massacre at Wounded Knee, in South Dakota, ended Sioux resistance.

1891 Red River Valley University opened (Wahpeton), now Wesley College at Grand Forks.

1893 Industrial school opened at Ellendale.

1897 First public library (Grafton). Red River Valley flooded.

1901 First state pure foods law passed.

1903 State school of science opened at Wahpeton.

1904 School for mentally retarded opened at Grafton.

1905 Historical Society of North Dakota became a state agency through legislative action.

1907 School of forestry opened at Bottineau.

1909 First child labor law enacted. State Library Commission (now State Library) created.

1910 First airplane flight in the state.

1911 First motor vehicle registration.

1913 Normal school opened at Minot. State Highway Commission created.

1915 Nonpartisan League organized.

1918 Seven initiated amendments, basis of Nonpartisan League platform, approved by electorate. Normal school opened at Dickinson. About 2,700 North Dakotans died in the Spanish Influenza epidemic.

1919 Bank of North Dakota established. Industrial Commission created.

1920 State mill and elevator built at Grand Forks.

1922 WDAY, first radio station (Fargo). First bus line began operation.

1928 Air mail service opened in the state.

1929 Drouth of the Thirties began.

1930 State capitol destroyed by fire. State reached peak population of 680,845.

1932 Cornerstone of new capitol laid. Prohibition clause of state constitution repealed. International Peace Garden established.

1933 New capitol completed.

1936 Only 34 percent of wheat acreage harvested. President Franklin D. Roosevelt visited drouth areas of state. Referendum legalized sale of liquor in the state. Last commercial boat retired from Missouri.

1940 North Dakota National Guard state staff ordered into federal military service.

1941 Several divisions of North Dakota National Guard ordered into service.

1943 North Dakota led all states in per capita war bond sales.

1947 Actual construction of Garrison Dam began. Theodore Roosevelt National Memorial Park established.

1950 Garrison Dam completed in July.

1951 Oil discovered (Tioga).

1952 Largest farm year on record in state.

1953 President Dwight D. Eisenhower spoke at Garrison Dam closure ceremonies. First television station (Minot). Only jewel-bearing plant in U. S. opened at Rolla.

1954 First large petroleum refinery dedicated at Mandan.

1964 John Burke statue placed in national Hall of Fame. North America's tallest structure (a 2,063-foot television tower) constructed near Mayville.

1967 Garrison Dam Reservoir officially named Lake Sakakawea.

1970 North Dakota was the first state to comply with the Clean Air Act.

1972 The only Omega station in North America established near LaMoure.

1977 North Dakota was the first in the nation to open Interstate Highway to traffic.

1989 North Dakota celebrated 100 years of statehood with "The Party of the Century."

1990 Miss Brynhild Haugland retired after 52 years of service in the North Dakota legislature. She was the nation's longest-serving state lawmaker.

INDEX

Abercrombie, John—40
Alliance (Farmers')—108
American Fur Company—28, 30, 36
American Society of Equity—108
Anson Northrop—40-41
Arikara Indians—7, 22, 23, 25-27
Arkertarnasher—22
Assiniboin Indians—7, 23, 25, 32
Astor, John Jacob—28
Audubon, John—32
Aviation—99-100
Barnard, Rev. Alonzo—38
Battles (Indian): Badlands—52,54; Custer—66-67; Killdeer Mountain—52; Little Bighorn—66-67; Whitestone Hill—51; Wounded Knee—85
Beadle, William Henry Harrison—83
Belcourt, George—39
Benteen, Frederick—66
Big White—24, 26-27
Bismarck **Tribune**—69
Black Hills gold—64, 65
Bodmer, Karl—31
Bonanza wheat farms—60-61
Bottineau, Charles—58-59
Boundary (International)—26
Buffalo—4, 5, 34-35, 61-62, 63, 72, 89
Bullboat—6, 25
Burbank, J. C. and Company—41
Burke, John—108
Burleigh, Walter A.—42
Calhoun, James E.—26
Cameahwait—24
Canfield, E. M.—100
Capitol: cornerstone laying (Territorial, Bismarck)—115; destroyed by fire—115; new—115, 117; removal from Yankton—82-83
Cass, George W.—60
Catlin, George—31
Cattlemen's Associations—81
Cavileer, Charles T.—39, 40
Chaboillez, Charles—18-19
Champlain, Samuel—14
Charbonneau, Toussaint—23, 24
Cheyenne Indians—64, 66
Chippewa Indians—9-10, 119
Christiansen, John—74-75
Coal—113
Cody, Buffalo Bill—84
Colleges and universities—104-107
Colter, John—24, 25
Commanche (horse)—68
Constitutional Convention (North Dakota)—86
Cortez, Hernando—9
Crazy Horse—66, 84
Crook, George—66
Curley—68
Custer Battle—66-67; reported—69
Custer, George Armstrong—64, 65, 66
Custer's Black Hills Expedition—64
Custom House Gang—82
Dakota Assembly—44
Dakota Indians, see Sioux Indians
Dakota Territory—42, 44, 56, 73
Dalrymple, Oliver—60, 101
D'Eglise—17
De Mores, Marquis—79-80
Depression, the Great—110-111, 115
De Smet, Father Pierre Jean—32
Dill, Daniel J.—54, 55
Dilts, Jefferson—55
Dorman, Dewey—99

Douglas, Lord (See Selkirk, Earl of)
Drift Prairie—1, 2
Education—102-107
Eielson, Carl Ben—100
Emmons, James A.—65
Evans, John—18
Expeditions: Custer's Black Hills—64; Custer's Seventh Cavalry against Sioux—65, 66, 67; Lewis and Clark—21-24, 26, 27; Major Long's—26; Sibley's—49-50; Sully's (1863)—49, 50; Sully's (1864)—51-54; Woods'—39; Yellowstone—27
Far West, The—66, 68, 69
Farm Bureau—109-110
Farm Holiday Association—110
Farm organizations—108, 110
Farmers' Union—107, 109, 110
Farming—107-111, 117-118
First Yellowstone Expedition—27
Firsts in North Dakota: airplane flight—99; airplane in state—99; auto race—96; basketball team—92; broadcasting—102; church bell—39; farmer—58; flour mill—39; football team—92; governor—87; melodeon—38; newspaper—101; one-room frame schoolhouse—103; postmaster—39, 100; printing press—38; school—102; train—59; telephone—101; television—102
Fisk, James L.—54, 55
Fisk Wagon Trains—54, 55
Fort Abercrombie—39, 40, 48, 58
Fort Abraham Lincoln—66, 69
Fort Benton—45
Fort Berthold Indian Reservation—70, 112, 114
Fort Buford—58
Fort Clark—30
Fort Daer—34
Fort Dilts—55
Fort Douglas—34
Fort Garry—39
Fort Lisa—26
Fort Mandan—22, 23, 24
Fort Pambian—19
Fort Pembina—19
Fort Ransom—58
Fort Rice—51, 55, 58
Fort Stevenson—58
Fort Totten—58
Fort Totten Indian Reservation—114
Fort Union—28, 30
Fort Yates—58
Four Bears—27
Freighter, The—41
Fremont, John C.—36
Fulton, Robert—27
Fur trade—14-18, 19-20
Garrison Dam—111-112
Geographical center of North America—118
Ghost Dance—84, 85
Gibbon, John—66
Gold: in Black Hills—64; in Montana—45
Goldseekers—45, 54-55
Gore, Sir George—32
Grandin Farms—61
Grandmother River (Missouri)
Grange, The—108
Grant, Ulysses S.—83
Great Northern Railway—40, 70-71
Hall, C. L.—112
Haynes, Frank Jay—102
Heerman, Edward—77
Henry, Alexander the Younger—19-20
Hidatsa Indians—7, 22, 33
Hill, James J.—70-71
Hills, Walter—48
Hjelm-Hansen, Paul—74
Homestead Act—44

Homesteading—59, 70, 71-73, 87-89
House, E. A.—51
Houston, David Henderson—102
Hoxey, Archie—99
Hudson, Henry—14
Hudson's Bay Company—20, 26, 34, 59
International boundary—26
Jayne, William—42, 44
Jusseaume, Rene—17, 23
Keelboats—21-22, 25
Kellogg, Mark—69
Kelly, Mrs. Fanny—55
Kipp, James—27, 28, 30
Kittson, Norman W.—38, 39, 40, 70
Klingensmith, Florence—100
Kroeze, Dr. Barend—104
Lake Agassiz—1
Lake Jessie—50
Lake Sakakawea—112, 118
La Salle, Robert—14
Lewis and Clark Expedition—21-24, 25, 28, 113
Lignite coal—113
Like-a-Fishhook Village—33, 112
Liquor and Indians: 19, 28, 30, 46
Lisa, Manuel—25-26
Little Crow—47
Long, Stephen H.—26
Long's Expedition—26, 36
"Longhorns"—62, 63, 77
Lottery—86
Lounsberry, Clement A.—69, 101
Mackinaw boats—25
Mail—100, 101
Mandan Indians—7, 22, 25, 32-33
Manufacturing—118
Marquis de Mores—79-80
Marsh, Grant—66, 68
"Martyrs of St. Joe"—38
Maximilian, Prince—31
McGoey, Tom—99, 100
McKay, James—17, 18
McKenzie, Alexander—83, 108
McKenzie, Kenneth—28, 30
McLaughlin, James—85
Metis—26, 34, 36, 38, 100
Miller, John—87
Milwaukee Railway—71
Minnie-H, The—77
Missouri Fur Company—26
Missouri Plateau—1. 2
Missouri River—25, 36, 77, 111-112
Missouri steamers—96
Navigation: of Missouri—25, 27, 30, 31, 77; of Red—40, 41, 77; of other rivers—77
New Salem—75
Newspapers, early—90, 91, 101
Nicollet, Jean N.—36
Nicollet's Survey—36
Nonpartisan League—109
Northern Pacific Railway—59-60
Northrop, Anson—40-41
North-West Company—18, 19, 34
Oil—113-114
Omega station—118
Omnibus Bill—83
Palliser, John—32
Park River—19-20
Peace Garden—117
Pembina—19, 20, 34, 36, 39, 44, 100, 102, 103
Pembina Hunt, Hunters—34-35
Pirogues—25
"Plenty Snow Winter"—79
Populists—108

Prairie fires—89
Prince Maximilian—31
Prohibition—86
Pryor, Nathaniel—26
Railways—107-108; Great Northern—70-71; land grants—59; Milwaukee—71; Northern Pacific—59-60; Soo—71 Ranching—62-63; 77-79; 87
Red Messiah—87
Red River Carts—20, 26, 36, 40, 96
Red River Cartways—36, 38
Red River steamers—96
Red Tomahawk—85
Reno, Marcus A.—66
Roberts, Vern—100
Rolette, Joe—36, 38, 39, 40, 44
Roosevelt, Theodore—81-82
St. Joseph (Walhalla)—38
St. Peter, The—32
Sakakawea—23, 24; Lake—112, 118
Schools—102-107
Second Yellowstone Expedition—27
Selkirk, Earl of—34
Selkirkers—34, 39
Shanties, claim—88
Shoshone Indians—23, 24
Sibley Expedition—49-50
Sibley, Henry Hastings—47
Sioux Indians—7, 22, 27, 32, 33, 44, 45, 52, 64, 66 Sioux Uprising—47-48
Sitting Bull—66, 69, 83, 84, 85, 86
Smallpox epidemics—32-33
Sodhouses—88
Stagecoaches—40, 96
Standing Rock Indian Reservation—85, 114
Statehood—86, 87
Stevens, Isaac Ingalls—39
Stevens Railway Survey—39
Stickney, Dr. Hugo—82
Stoneboats—89, 96
Stutsman, Enos—44
Sully, Alfred—49, 50
Sully Expedition of 1863—49; of 1864—51-54
Surveys: Long's—36; Nicollet's—36; Stevens'—39-40; Thompson's—18, 19
Telegraph—101
Telephone—101, 102
Television—102
Terry, Alfred—66
Thompson, David—18, 19
Thordarson, T. W.—107
Thorlakson, Rev. Pall—73-74
Timber Culture Act—59
Townley, Arthur C.—109, 113
Townsite companies—56
Traffic, early regulations—96
Turtle Mountain Indian Reservation—114, 119
Vanderhorck, John—48
Verendrye, Pierre de la and sons—16-17
Vigilantes—78
Villard, Henry—83
Voyageurs—16
Weiser, Dr. Josiah S.—50
"Wheeling"—96
Whipple, Henry Benjamin—47
Wild life in early times—2, 19
Winter of 1886-1887—79
Woodhawks—31, 56
Woods, Samuel—39
Woods' Expedition—39
Wounded Knee, Battle of—85
Yankton—42, 49, 82
Yellowstone, The—30, 31
Yellowstone Expeditions—27

DAKOTA GOVERNORS

Dakota Territory, 1861-1889

William Jayne, 1861-1863
Newton Edmunds, 1863-1866
Andrew J. Faulk, 1866-1869
John A. Burbank, 1869-1874
John L. Pennington, 1874-1878
William A. Howard, 1878-1880 (Died in office, April 10, 1880) Nehemiah G. Ordway, 1880-1884
Gilbert A. Pierce, 1884-1887
Louis K. Church, 1887-1889
Arthur C. Mellette, 1889

North Dakota

John Miller, 1889-1890
Andrew H. Burke, 1891-1892
Eli C. Shortridge, 1893-1894
Roger Allin, 1895-1896
Frank A. Briggs, 1897-1898 (Died, August 8, 1898)
Joseph M. Devine served unexpired term of Briggs, 1898 Fred B. Fancher, 1899-1900
Frank White, 1901-1904
E. Y. Sarles, 1905-1906
John Burke, 1907-1912
Louis B. Hanna, 1913-1916
Lynn J. Frazier, 1917-1921 (Recalled, October 28, 1921) R. A. Nestos, 1921-1924
A. G. Sorlie, 1925-1928 (Died August 28, 1928)
Walter Maddock served unexpired term, 1928
George Shafer, 1929-1932
William Langer, 1933-1934 (Removed, July 17, 1934)
Ole H. Olson served unexpired term, 1934
Thomas H. Moodie, 1935 (Removed, February 16, 1935) Walter Welford served unexpired term, 1935-1936
William Langer, 1937-1938
John Moses, 1939-1944
Fred G. Aandahl, 1945-1950
Norman Brunsdale, 1951-1856
John E. Davis, 1957-1960
William L. Guy, 1961-1972
Arthur Link, 1973-1980
Allen I. Olson, 1981-1984
George A. Sinner, 1985—

HISTORIC PLACES TO SEE

There are 101 local and county historical societies in the state and 78 of these have museums of some kind. Inquire locally for specific directions to historic sites.

Buffalo Creek marker   Point where General Henry H. Sibley's expedition of 3300 soldiers and 200 wagons crossed on August 16, 1863, on return to Minnesota. Cass County. Buffalo vicinity.

Burman headstone marks place where Dr. Josiah S. Weiser was shot by Indians, July 24, 1863. This precipitated the Battle of Big Mound. Kidder County.

Camp Arnold headstones honor memory of two Sibley Expedition soldiers who died at the August 14, 1863, campsite. Barnes County.

Camp Atchinson marker   Field base of 1863 Sibley Expedition. Griggs County.

Camp Corning marker   July 16-17 campsite of 1863 Sibley Expedition Barnes County. Dazey vicinity.

Camp Grant marker   July 23rd campsite of Sibley Expedition. Stutsman County. Woodworth vicinity.

Camp Hancock   Camp Greeley (1872) military installation to protect men building the Northern Pacific railway. Camp's name later changed to Hancock. Served as supply depot for Fort Abraham Lincoln and posts further west. Post was decommissioned in 1894, then used by Bismarck Weather Station until 1940, by U. S. Soil Conservation Service until 1949. Headquarters building still stands and serves as local museum. Site also has a 1909 Northern Pacific Railway steam locomotive and the 1885 Bread of Life Episcopal Church. In downtown Bismarck.

Camp Sheardown marker   July 14-15 camp of 1863 Sibley Expedition. Barnes County. Valley City area.

Camp Weiser marker   July 13-14 camp of 1863 Sibley Expeditio. Barnes County. Kathryn vicinity.

Cannonball Stage Station marker Site of fifth stagecoach stop from Bismarck to the Black Hills, 1877-1880. Picnic shelters, water, park on bank of Cannonball River. Grant County. Carson area.

Chaska marker   Site of Camp Banks, August 2nd campsite of Sibley Expedition. Chaska, an Indian scout, died and was buried in the fortification ditch surrounding the campsite. Burleigh County. Driscoll vicinity.

Chateau de Mores   26-room 19th century summer home of the Marquis and Marquise de Mores. Now historic house museum containing many original furnishings and personal belongings of the de Mores family. Tours during summer months. Near Medora, Billings County.

David Thompson Memorial A large, spherical, granite memorial honoring the geographer who made first reliable map of the Souris River area. McHenry County. Near Verendrye.

de Mores Packing Plant Tall brick chimney marks place where was once the packing plant, slaughterhouse, three ice houses, several outbuildings, a railroad spur track, and a corral owned and operated by the Marquis de Mores. On west edge of Medora, the town established by the Duke. His statue stands in the town.

Double Ditch Indian Village   Ruins of a large Mandan earthlodge village. Site has a stone shelter. Burleigh County.

Eielson House, home of Carl Ben Eielson. In Hatton.

Fort Abercrombie Military post (1857-1878). First U. S. military fort in North Dakota. Stage stop. Besieged by Indians during the Sioux Uprising. One original building. Reconstructed blockhouses and palisade wall. Richland County. Eastern edge of Abercrombie.

Fort Abraham Lincoln State Park Includes On-a-Slant Mandan earthlodge village site; the blockhouses of Fort McKeen (1872-1891); the infantry post grounds of Fort Lincoln (1873-1891); the recently restored Custer House. Museum-visitor center. Morton County. Four miles south of Mandan, Highway 1806.

Fort Buford Military post (1866-1895) Original stone powder magazine, post cemetery, officers' building now housing a museum. Williams County, Williston area.

Fort Clark Site of American Fur Company trading post (1830-1831). Contains foundations of fort structure, remains of earthlodge village, and large native burial ground. Tours. Resident site supervisor. Open all year. Mercer County. Stanton vicinity.

Fort Dilts markers and memorials Site of sod-walled fortification built by James L. Fisk party of goldseekers attacked by Sioux Indians in September, 1864. Bowman County. Rhame vicinity.

Fort Mandan interpretive markers Near where the Lewis and Clark winter fort was built, 1804-1895. McLean County. (A reconstruction of Fort Mandan, operated by McLean County Historical Society, is 4 miles west of Washburn.) McLean County.

Fort Ransom Site of military post built in 1867. Protected overland travelers until it was decommissioned in 1872. Building locations, remains of sod and log wall discernible. Ransom County. Fort Ransom vicinity.

Fort Rice markers Site of military fort (1864-1877). Morton County. Near town of Fort Rice.

Fort Seward site Military post to replace Fort Ransom (1872). Protected crews building Northern Pacific Railroad. Decommissioned in 1877. Foundations and basements of some buildings remain visible. Stutsman County, northwest of Jamestown.

Fort Totten Military post (1867-1890). Brick buildings are well-preserved. Original buildings now house a museum and theatre. Benson County. Near town of Fort Totten.

Gingras Trading Post Established by Metis trader, Antoine Gingras, in the 1840s. His hand-hewn log store and home have been restored. Pembina County. Walhalla vicinity.

Governor's Mansion (former) Victorian house built in 1884 by Asa Fisher. The state bought it for the governor's mansion in 1893 and from that time until 1960, 23 governors and their families lived in it. Open for tours, summers. Bismarck, Fourth Street and Eighth Avenue.

Huff Indian Village Site Ruins of large rectangular earthlodge dwellings believed occupied by Mandan Indians during fifteenth century. Morton County. Huff vicinity.

Killdeer Battlefield marker Commemorates battle fought July 28, 1864, between General Alfred Sully's troops and Sioux Indians. Dunn County. Killdeer vicinity.

Kittson's Trading Post Built by Norman Kittson in St. Joseph, the trading post building is one of the oldest buildings in the state. Town was revived and renamed Wallhalla. Pembina County.

Lake Jessie In 1839, the Nicollet-Fremont expedition camped here. It was also the site of camping by the Isaac Stevens railway survey party, and by James L. Fisk and his goldseekers. Griggs County.

McPhail's Butte marker Site from which Colonel Samuel McPhail directed First Minnesota Rangers in the Battle of Big Mound, July 24, 1863, during Sibley Expedition. Kidder County.

Menoken Indian Village Site Remains of a prehistoric earthlodge village surrounded by fortification ditch. Burleigh County. Menoken vicinity.

Miner, Hazel, memorial Honors girl who sacrificed her life to save her younger brother and sister in a blizzard. Courthouse grounds, Center.

Molander Indian Village Site Preserves remains of a large prehistoric earthlodge village with fortification ditch. Oliver County. Price vicinity.

Palmer's Spring Site of a way station on Fort Totten-Fort Stevenson Trail. A mail wagon and escort were attacked here by Sioux Indians; three soldiers were killed, and two escaped. Frank Palmer and a soldier teamster were watering Palmer's horse at the spring, were out of sight and Palmer rode to Fort Totten for help. Unmarked, but trail ruts are visible near the spring. Benson County. Esmond area.

Pembina Charles Chaboillez built his trading post here in 1797, then Alexander Henry the Younger established the Northwest Company's post here in 1801. First non-Indian child was born here in 1802, daughter of Henry's Negro servant, Pierre Bonza. First church and school (1818), first post office(1849), and first customs office (1851). Museum interprets area history. Pembina County. City of Pembina.

Sitting Bull Monument Original grave of Hunkpapa Sioux leader. Sioux County. Town of Fort Yates.

Steamboat Warehouse marker Site of a warehouse built by Northern Pacific Railroad for trans-shipment of goods between steamboats and trains. Dock area, west edge of Bismarck.

Sully's Corral Site of base camp established by General Alfred Sully while his army escorted 600 civilians enroute to Montana gold mines. Rifle pits visible. Stark County. Richardton vicinity.

Fort Union National Historic Site. Famous fur-trade post of John Jacob Astor's American Fur Company (1828-1867). Reconstructed 17-foot high palisade walls, the elegant Bourgeois House, two fieldstone bastions, trade house, and flag pole. Reconstruction continues. Williams County. Southwest of Williston.

Whitestone Hill Battlefield September 3, 1863, General Alfred Sully's troops fought Sioux Indians here. Site now includes a small museum, campground, graveyard, marker, and a monument. Dickey County. Merricourt area.

Writing Rock Two large boulders here bear Indian pictographs. Protected by an enclosed shelter. Divide County. Grenora vicinity.

Note: There are other historic sites that are unmarked, and some are on private property.

SOURCES FOR ILLUSTRATIONS

Author—2, 3, 49, 59, 80, 84, 167
American Museum of Natural History, New York—6
Armstrong, Moses K.—67, 70, 73
BHG, INC., Garrison—181
Bismarck **Tribune**—100, 111
Bluemle, John P., ND assistant geologist—2
Caniff, Walter A.—178, 179
Concordia College Office of Communications—28
Farm Security Administration—186, 201, 202, 206, 207
Frank Leslie's **Illustrated Newspaper**—83
Green, Sheldon—66, 78
Greater North Dakota Association—203
Greater Rugby Area Chamber of Commerce—213
Harper's Monthly Magazine—57
Hudson's Bay Company—65
Independent Farmer & Fireside Companion—91
International Peace Garden—211, 212
Jefferson National Expansion Museum, St. Louis, Missouri—38
Johnson, M. A.—209
Jerdee, Rebecca—10, 11, 16, 17, 22-26, 29
Jessen's Weekly, Fairbanks, Alaska—180
The Kenmare **News**—214
Masseth, George Jr.—128
Melin, Raymond—61
Minnesota Historical Society—33, 72, 75, 76, 117, 118
Montana Historical Society—43, 161
North Dakota Institute for Regional Studies—106, 156
Northwest Magazine—92
Opsal, Don—30
Peters, John—77
Putney, Hilda—82
Quebec Service de Cine-Photographic—32
Red River Valley Potato Growers Association—1
Sebens, W. P.—196
Schoenhut, Mrs. William—152
Sletto, Josephine—98
Smithsonian Institute—5, 7-9, 19, 20, 27, 52, 53, 93
South Dakota Historical Society—95, 99
Soil Conservation Service—200
State Historical Society of North Dakota—12-15, 18, 21, 31, 34-37, 39-42, 44-48, 50, 51, 54-56, 58, 60, 62-64, 68, 69, 71, 74, 79, 81, 85-90, 94, 96, 97, 101-105, 107-110, 112-116, 119-127, 129-133, 135-140, 142-151, 153-155, 157-160, 162-166, 168-177, 182-185, 187-192, 194, 197-199, 205, 208, 210, 78A
State School for the Deaf—193
University of Illinois Library—134
U. S. Army Corps of Engineers—204
U. S. National Park Service—4, 141

ACKNOWLEDGEMENTS

This informal history of North Dakota was written for growing-up youngsters and for tired adults who like to read after a day of work. In his youth, the author had no such book available to him. So, for a long time, he failed to appreciate the rich and colorful fibre woven through the historical heritage of his native state.

It is thirty-five years ago that I first began researching the history of North Dakota. The early years culminated in the publication of my **Story of North Dakota** in 1963. The response from that book was very gratifying.

Much of the present volume is based on the research for that first book and I, therefore, wish to acknowledge the help and support given by several key persons in producing that book:

Russell Reid, superintendent of the State Historical Society of North Dakota; Mrs. Florence Davis, the Society librarian, and Miss Margaret Rose who succeeded Mrs. Davis; and Mrs. Martha Wetmore, the Society newspaper archivist, back in those pre-microfilm days when newspapers were kept full size in large bound volumes.

Like Mrs. Davis, Miss Clara A. Richards, the librarian at the Masonic Grand Lodge Library in Fargo, was a veritable encyclopedia of North Dakota lore and gave valuable support. Mrs. C. B. Hay and Mrs. Paul Nerhus, assistant librarians, spared no effort to help.

Always remembered will be the help given by Miss Gena A. Bakken, reference librarian at the State Library Commission, Bismarck.

The North Dakota Institute for Regional Studies, NDSU, was always cooperative, and particularly generous in the loan of photographs.

And there were individuals who assisted in various ways. At Fargo, James B. Connolly and David J. Ringstad; at Alexandia, Minnesota, John Whelan, David Dziuk, Ray Rueter, Mrs. Chester J. Hustad, Don Opsal, my wife Beverly, daughter Becky, and son Stan.

In preparing the present volume of **Story of the Peace Garden State** I owe thanks to James A. Davis, reference specialist; Gerald A. Newborg, state archivist; Larry Remele, state historian and managing editor of **North Dakota History**; Todd Strand, photo archivist, all of the State Historical Society of North Dakota staff.

My thanks to the staff of the Alexandria Public Library, particularly Terri Andreen and Patricia Conroy.

I asked several people to read portions of the original computer copy critically and these gave such assistance: Doris Sperling, Susan Kelly-Weinauer, Bruce Kelly, my daughters Linda and Solveig. At the Washington School in Fargo, Esther Hornbacher and Nancy Budish read the entire manuscript to their fourth-grade classes; at the Edison School in Minot, Kathleen Froeber read portions to her fourth-grade class; and at Sterling, Molly Hoff read early chapters to her upper grades students.

Special thanks go to my wife Beverly for her careful reading of final copy and to my son Stan for the benefits of his newspaper publishing expertise. Nor can I omit Al Skaar and Laurie Groothuis for their technical advice.

May those who so generously gave of their time and energy in this project find joy in the finished product.

Erling Nicolai Rolfsrud
Route 1, Box 104
Farwell, Minnesota 56327